The Negro Challenge to the Business Community

The Negro Challenge to the Business Community

EDITED BY ELI GINZBERG

McGRAW-HILL BOOK COMPANY
New York   San Francisco   Toronto   London

Preface

This book presents the highlights of a conference held at Arden House on January 15 to 17, 1964, under the auspices of the Executive Program of the Graduate School of Business, Columbia University. The impetus to hold the conference came from Mr. Oscar Cohen of the Anti-Defamation League, and all the details were worked out by Mr. Hoke Simpson, Director of the Executive Program. I served as Technical Director and was assisted by four resource personnel: Dr. Dale Hiestand, Research Associate of the Conservation of Human Resources Project, Columbia University; Dr. John G. Feild, Consultant to the Eleanor Roosevelt Foundation; Mr. Joseph P. Lyford, Information Officer and Director of the New York Office of The Fund for the Republic, Inc., of the Center for the Study of Democratic Institutions, Santa Barbara, California; and Mr. Oscar Cohen.

The primary objective of the conference was educational. The large number of corporations that sent representatives confirmed the sponsors' conviction that it would be constructive for leaders of the business community to have an opportunity to gain new perspective on the aspirations and actions of Negroes as they seek to participate more fully in the economy and society. The formal presentations that constitute the heart of this volume were an attempt to provide this perspective.

A second objective of the conference was to encourage the participants to discuss the complex facets of the problem among themselves and to exchange information and opinions about the ways in which business might contribute to constructive resolutions. To encourage free and open discussion, the participants were assured that their individual contributions would be off the record.

Nevertheless, the participants felt that since a considerable amount of useful information had been developed in the discussion groups it would be desirable to make the proceedings available to the business community at large, subject only to safeguarding the anonymity of the speakers and of the organizations.

At the final session of the conference, a brief report was made of the highlights developed in each of the discussion groups. This was recorded and is here included without identification. Also included are the summary observations of the resource personnel, of whom one was assigned to each of the four discussion groups.

The major task of turning the tapes into finished manuscript was carried by Ruth Szold Ginzberg. Without sacrificing important content, she was able to transform the loose sentences of speeches into readable prose.

Eli Ginzberg

Contents

AMERICAN DEMOCRACY AND THE NEGRO

Eli Ginzberg

This presentation will attempt to answer three questions: How did we get to where we are? Where are we now? And what alternatives do we face?

The answer to the first question has relevance for the second and third. How did we get here? My own examination of this question goes back to 1956, when I wrote a little book, *The Negro Potential*. At that time I developed a few answers and then put the problem to one side. I stayed interested, however, in what was happening with the nation's human resources as a whole and with minority problems in particular, and I continued to be disturbed throughout that period by an underlying awareness that I did not understand how we had arrived at our present position.

One conspicuous strength of American democracy has been its ability to take all kinds of people, put them through similar experiences, and absorb the end products with little difficulty.

But the Negro, who arrived in America in 1619 and therefore has been here longer than the Pilgrims, has not been absorbed by our democracy. His experience has been different from that of all other groups.

This fact, inexplicable on the surface, proved to be so disturbing that I began, about three years ago, to work on it. I started at the beginning of our history in order to see this piece of history in perspective. With a young and very able collaborator, Alfred Eichner, I sought to capture the reasons for this differential experience. The result of our study is a book, *The Troublesome Presence*, which carries the subtitle *American Democracy and the Negro*. The title comes from Lincoln's eulogy of his idol, Henry Clay, and refers to the presence of the *free* Negro in America. The book, with its emphasis upon the broad historical picture and upon some economic and political facets of the subject, provides a useful frame for a discussion of our first question —how did we get here? It suggests, further, that the answer to the question is threefold: By accident, by intent, and by neglect.

Let me illustrate each in turn. The Negro came to the United States initially by accident. He arrived in Colonial America through no deliberate plan but because a Dutch man-of-war carrying Negroes who had been bought in the West Indies happened to land in Jamestown. At that time the British had had little or no experience or contact with Africans. Unlike the Spanish and the Portuguese, who had lived in the Mediterranean world, they knew nothing about Negroes.

The British colonists in Virginia confronted persons such as they had never seen, strange, black people who spoke no European tongue and had no customs or religion in common with Englishmen or other Europeans. The Negroes had been demoralized by the brutal trek from inland Africa to the coast and were further demoralized by the journey across the Atlantic. They seemed not to belong to the human species, at least not to any segment familiar to the British. No question about it, these Negroes scared the colonists.

The first case on record involving a Negro appears in the Jamestown annals of 1630, where it is recorded that a white man was punished by the assembly in Jamestown for sleeping with a Negro woman. The decision indicates that the community was appalled by the notion that there could be close relationships between white and black. From the very start, then, the colonists had no intention of integrating the Negro into their community. The British colonists, who came from a culture that had had no experience with slavery, instituted slavery for Negroes and basically only for Negroes. They tried it for a short while with Indians, but it didn't work, and before very long, enslavement of Indians was prohibited.

Because they could not conceive of living cheek by jowl with free Negroes, the British community sought to develop some method of social control over these strangers in their midst. Englishmen had come to America to build a new society, and slavery was introduced to protect that nascent society. It evolved as a method of enabling the colonists to live with Negroes, not originally as a system of economic exploitation.

But before long, the expansion of Southern agriculture made necessary the recruitment of large numbers of laborers. White farm laborers were available, but they were not reliable hired help; they wanted to farm land of their own. For a capitalistically successful plantation system, therefore, Negro labor became not only useful but essential. In fact, from around 1700, Negro labor alone made possible the expansion of Southern plantations. Large-scale recruiting of white indentured servants—about 80 per cent of all Britishers who emigrated came under some kind of labor contract—was expensive. White immigrants required better clothing, better food, and even wages! The colonists could entice more and more white people to come only if they were willing to provide attractive wages and working conditions.

With Negro slaves, however, they did not have to provide more than a minimum. The entire procedure operated differently. Negroes "immigrated" after having been captured and traded.

Therefore, there was no need to lighten the conditions of their servitude. They became a minority that was soon completely under the control of the white majority. This was the first step in regularizing the relations between American democracy and the Negro. And as often happens, the first step had important consequences.

The second answer to our first question, how did we get here, relates to intent. The first significant attempt to study the relationship between Negro and white Americans was made in the early 1940s when the Swedish economist Gunnar Myrdal published his famous study, *An American Dilemma*. The Carnegie Corporation had asked a Swedish economist to study the problem because it believed that any American student would be prejudiced. Myrdal, a distinguished social scientist from a country with no minorities and no colonial possessions, was their choice, and his study became the first comprehensive socio-economic-political analysis of the Negro minority in the United States, cast largely in terms of developments since World War I. Myrdal's imaginative conclusion from his large-scale study was that there had been a continuing conflict between our conscience and our behavior—that is, the Declaration of Independence had proclaimed that all men are created equal, but we had been treating the Negro as if he were *not* equal.

In my opinion, Myrdal was wrong. No basic conflict ever existed between our conscience and our behavior because we did not include the Negro in our original commitment. "All men" meant "all white men." The Negro was excluded. Chief Justice Taney was legally correct, although he may have been politically unwise, when he said in the Dred Scott decision that at the time of the Revolution the law did not bestow citizenship on the Negro American. A state might grant citizenship to a Negro, he held, but the Founding Fathers had not included him within the polity and surely not as a full-fledged member.

We know that Jefferson considered assimilation impossible. He wanted to send 500,000 Negroes back to Africa and in their place import an equal number of white persons. There was, in his opinion, no resolution of the Negro problem except by an exchange of populations. This was the only solution recommended by the man who drafted the Declaration of Independence.

From George Washington to William Howard Taft, no president of the United States, not even Lincoln, had any answer for the Negro in the United States other than colonization or some variant thereof. George Washington once promised General Lafayette personally to help underwrite an experimental colonization scheme for American Negroes in the West Indies. Shortly after his election to the presidency, William Howard Taft, who considered himself free of any kind of color prejudice, told a Negro college audience in North Carolina that they had no future in this country, that they should go back to Africa. If they stayed here, he said, they would remain peasants. And Taft was the President who devoted a good part of his inaugural address to an assessment of the Negro problem in the United States.

In the middle of the Civil War Lincoln went to the Congress and obtained funds for the colonization of slaves who had recently been freed. He attempted first to develop a colony in Panama and when that failed, he supported a scheme in Haiti. Six weeks before Lincoln died he asked Major General Butler, Chief of Logistics for the Union Army, to explore the rate at which Negroes could be sent abroad if use were made of all naval and civilian shipping. Butler reported back to the effect that not much could be accomplished because Negroes were being born at a rate faster than the numbers that could be shipped out.

These excerpts from our history indicate that the colonization movement was not started or supported by rabid Southerners with extreme positions. The plan had the support of the great leaders of American democracy, Washington, Jefferson, and Lincoln.

This does not imply that all Americans have always been

insensitive to or pessimistic about finding a constructive solution to the Negro problem. The Quakers early attacked slavery. But the clearest and most unequivocal indication about the mood of the new nation is reflected in the Constitution, the basic law of the land. Three, and only three, propositions in the Constitution dealt with the Negro. One stipulated that the Congress of the United States could not interfere with the importation of slaves for twenty years. Not that importation had to stop at the end of twenty years, but Congress could not interfere until then. The second proposition provided that the Federal government could use its power to return escaped slaves to their masters. In this the Constitution treated slaves as property.

The third proposition related to the counting of the population to determine the allocation of seats in the House of Representatives. For this purpose, the Negro was to be counted as three-fifths of a man. As one reads the debates in the Constitutional Convention, it becomes clear that the Negro issue per se was unimportant. Some of the Northern delegates would have preferred different action and different wording, but few would have gone beyond abolishing the slave trade. Delegates from some of the middle states—Maryland, Delaware and Virginia—were more incensed about the failure to act on the slave trade than were New Englanders and New Yorkers. In short, at the time of the Constitutional Convention, white America—not just the Southern states, but white America—had no interest in and saw no possibility of bringing the panoply of American democracy over the Negro.

To shift focus, one year after the Civil War was under way, Lincoln told Horace Greeley that if the Union could be re-established without freeing a single slave, he would aim to do it. Certainly Lincoln believed that slavery was an evil, but he decided that, since ours was a constitutional government, the South had been guaranteed by the Constitution the right to hold slaves. Lincoln stood athwart only the *expansion* of slavery. And it was on the question of the expansion of slavery that the war was fought, since the irreconcilable issue was control of the West, which carried with it control of the nation.

Lincoln knew early and most Northerners soon came to understand that if slavery were permitted in the Western territories, settlement there of Northern whites would be foreclosed. Northern whites would be loath to move there; control of the West would be won by the South. On that issue—the control of the West—the war was fought. Even after the war began, many Northerners balked at calling slavery the issue. Members of an Illinois regiment proclaimed that they would prefer to stay in the fields until they were covered by moss than take any action that would help free the slaves.

When Lincoln issued the Emancipation Proclamation, which we recall freed slaves only in the states in rebellion, the legislature of the state from which he came, Illinois, drafted a memorial to the effect that it was the most dastardly act in the history of mankind. This was the mood of part of the North even at that late hour.

Of course, many Abolitionists under the leadership of such men as William Lloyd Garrison had long preached that slavery was immoral and un-Christian, and their agitation had undoubtedly helped bring on the war. But they considered slavery largely as an abstract institution. When slavery finally was eliminated as a result of the war, Frederick Douglass, the leader of the Negro community to the extent that one can speak of a Negro community at that time, understood that the ex-slaves, with neither education nor property, would need considerable and prolonged help if they were to be integrated successfully into the larger society. But at that crucial point, Garrison and his colleagues withdrew from the fray. With slavery abolished, they saw their work at an end. Most of them had little understanding of, or feeling for, the individual Negro.

To be sure, not all Americans had such little sympathy and understanding, but this was the dominant attitude even in Massachusetts, where Abigail Adams, the wife of our second president, found it necessary to personally nurse her sick old Negro servant because she could not get any white woman to help her.

Lincoln was a constitutionalist and a conservative. He believed that the South had the right to perpetuate the institution of slavery. But he did not believe that the Constitution gave the South the right to spread slavery to the new territories in the West. After the Southern states started to secede, he repeatedly stated that he would do nothing to interfere with the institution of slavery where it was established.

Although he tried to broaden the interpretation of the Declaration of Independence to include Negroes, Lincoln felt that as President of the United States he was not entitled to implement his personal views. He fought to maintain the integrity of the Union. The expansion of slavery, not slavery itself, would, he believed, hopelessly corrupt our democracy, but if he could build a wall around the South, slavery would eventually die out.

Few Northern leaders considered what might happen once the slaves were freed. Lincoln looked forward originally to a slow emancipation, to be completed only at the beginning of the next century. Thaddeus Stevens, who understood the preconditions for the social, economic and political integration of the Negro, believed that a revolution in the South would be necessary before the Negro could sink roots as a freedman. Hence, he initially opposed enfranchising the Negro, thinking that that ought to come second or third after economic security and educational gains.

For a short while after the Civil War, the North tried to help the Negro, not because Northerners were interested in the Negro as a human being, but because they did not want to forfeit the gains of having won the War. The fact that the Freedmen's Bureau was originally to cease operations one year after the end of hostilities reveals how completely the North misunderstood the magnitude of the problem it faced. Even after the act establishing the Bureau was amended, the Bureau remained in operation for only four years. The victorious North, at least its representatives in Congress, was unwilling to invest very much in helping the freed Negro, although individuals and missionary groups in the North went South and started to teach Negro children and adults during and after the war.

So much for intent. Now some comments about neglect: Although the government never intended to do much for the Negro, most of the benefits which did redound to the Negro were the result of fights among white groups. During the Revolutionary War, for example, the British had offered Negro slaves their freedom in return for fighting on their side. In response, George Washington, who had originally refused to take Negroes into the Colonial Army, reversed his position and accepted them. Again, during the Civil War, Lincoln originally refused to take Negroes into the Army. But when it became clear that failure to do so would aid the Southern cause, he shifted tack and accepted them. Again the Negroes benefited from the whites' fighting among themselves.

This recital of what the whites intended refers to the majority. There was always a minority, most of them deeply religious, who were disturbed by the slave trade, by slavery, and by the inhumanity of the nation's actions to the free Negro. But they were a small minority.

Booker T. Washington's famous speech at the 1895 Atlanta Exposition described the real plight of the Southern Negro. Ninety per cent of all Negroes were still living in the South, existing precariously by the grace of the Southerners, who felt little good will toward them. Meanwhile, the North had deserted the Negro. The South, now out of the main stream of American life, had given way to the Westward push of the country from New York to San Francisco. Thirty million immigrants were to come from Europe during these post-Civil War decades, pre-empting opportunities that otherwise would have been available to the Negro in the North or West. Had the North been interested in helping the Negro after the Civil War it would have provided opportunities for their migration out of the South;

it would have helped them obtain land in the West. But the North was not interested. Indeed, it sought to keep them in the South.

The fact that Northerners did not have to confront the situation head-on made it easier for the South to continue its oppressive ways. There was no television, no radio, and little good reporting. The plight of the Negro—even lynchings—wasn't news. President Theodore Roosevelt reflected the North's attitude when he remarked that while he did not condone lynching there were few alternative ways to protect white womanhood in the South. As a matter of fact, it was not the North but the white churchwomen of the South who finally put an end to lynching.

Another key fact in our history has been the controlling political power of the North and West together. The South alone has never had the votes to direct the nation. What has happened to the Negro, therefore, must reflect the attitudes and desires of the North and the West, for they have had the votes. But they were not interested. Until 1957, the Republican Middle West and West and the Southern white Democrats had a silent agreement to keep the Federal government out of race relations.

The national intent can also be read in the Supreme Court decisions towards the end of the nineteenth century, which were intended to restrict the scope of the Thirteenth, Fourteenth, and Fifteenth Amendments. The country was weary of racial friction and the Supreme Court sought to contribute to peace by handing the Negro back to the control and mercy of the Southern states.

In the history of American democracy vis-a-vis the Negro, the end of slavery marked the end of stage one. World War I was a second turning point, for it accelerated the movement of Negroes out of the South and into Northern industry. Four hundred thousand Negroes were drafted, and many of them saw service overseas. In their army service they saw a way of life they had never seen before. The postwar decade saw further mobility and progress, but the Great Depression wiped out many of these earlier gains.

World War II was the third, and in many ways most important, turning point. This time a postwar prosperity broadened and consolidated many of the wartime gains. Millions of Negroes were able to leave the South to come North, where they got jobs and lived reasonably well for the first time in their lives.

Another turning point was 1948. The Democratic platform in 1948 demonstrated for the first time in American history that the Negro had accumulated a significant degree of political power. With Truman's election, the Negro began to have some political leverage. During Truman's administration, desegregation in the armed services proceeded apace. And then Eisenhower, despite his conservatism, encouraged by the Supreme Court in its tradition-breaking decisions, introduced the first civil rights bill since Reconstruction.

Because Negroes today have political power and growing economic power, they also have the power to affect their situation. Twenty million Negroes do not, of course, constitute a homogeneous group. Some Southern rural Negroes are very poor and uneducated, as are many Southern urban Negroes. But many other Negroes are neither poor nor uneducated. In Houston, Negroes buy at retail annually over 500 million dollars; over 300 million in Atlanta; in New Orleans over 250 million. With that amount of purchasing power Negroes can get banks to treat them civilly; they can get salespeople in department stores to want to sell to them. Recent data reveal that there are about a million nonwhites on the West Coast, most of them Negroes. The income distribution of the nonwhite group is exactly the same as that of the white population in the South. In Chicago, one-third of the Negro families have more income than half of the white families.

We see that a concept of 20 million poverty-stricken, uneducated, socially disorganized human beings is unfounded. There are many middle-class Negro families and even a few Negro millionaires. Serious problems remain, of course. Many Negroes are poor, but so are many white persons; in fact there are many more poor white families than poor Negro families, although a higher proportion of all Negroes are poor.

In addition to the Negro's recently acquired political and economic power, another significant transformation has recently taken place. The Negro has decided to become directly involved in changing his relationships to the white community. The sit-ins heralded this transformation, which foreshadows the end of segregation, since those against whom discrimination has been practiced are no longer willing to be passive. A system of segregation can work only as long as those who are segregated are willing to tolerate it. When they decide to fight it, when they cause continuing disturbances, then the costs of maintaining the system outweigh the advantages of shoring it up. Picket lines put business in a turmoil; classes in school are disrupted; dissonance pervades the social system.

The Negro alone cannot change the fabric of the social structure, but his resistance and struggle to present inequities can encourage others to shift their position. This is the meaning back of the current civil rights struggle. The Negro stands a good chance of getting white America finally to grant him his constitutional rights.

To answer our third question, where do we go from here, we must first distinguish three centers: the rural South, the urban South, and the urban North. Fortunately most Negroes have left the rural South, as have many white people. Nevertheless, a number of Negroes and white people have remained, and it is not a good place to be. Public services are inadequate, jobs are scarce, and income is low. The Negro there must still worry about his personal security. If he stands up for his rights he may be permanently silenced. About one-quarter of the Negro population continues to live in the rural South. The urban South where a slightly higher proportion of Negroes live, is a better environment, for urban communities need peace and tranquility if they are to progress. Strong pressures therefore exist for granting an insistent minority its civil and political rights. The urban North, including the West—the home of almost half of the Negro population—faces the challenge of giving meaning to the political and civic freedom that the Negro possesses.

These are three different areas, three different sets of conditions, three different stages of adjustment. The rural South requires at a minimum some Federal protection of potential Negro voters. If Negro voters in the Southern cities learn to use their votes intelligently they can influence state legislatures to protect Negro rights in rural communities. But rural Negroes need protection and help in acquiring and using their franchise.

With regard to the second area, we cannot talk about the urban South as an entity. There are big differences between the situation confronting the urban Negro in Florida and that facing him in Virginia. Nevertheless, here, too, a major goal for Negroes is to attain their full political and civil rights. In 1882, a Southern white journalist and novelist by the name of George Washington Cable, a friend of Mark Twain, wrote perspicaciously that at the rate the racial problem was being handled we would get to the moon before we reached a solution.

A second goal for the Negro in the urban South should be to get a better share of the tax dollar and a better share of the public services, particularly access to better schools and health services. But most important is the question of jobs. Here improvement will come slowly, however, because the South is a manpower-surplus area. The Negro is thus twice handicapped because there are not enough jobs even for white people.

In the urban North, the Negro, despite his considerable gains in employment, seems to be pursued by an evil fate, for many of his gains are now being liquidated by automation. His breakthrough in semiskilled jobs came in the automobile industry, meat packing, steel, rubber, and other basic industries, where Negroes have recently been able to earn $2.50 to $3.00 an hour, which, with overtime, often brings weekly earnings up to $125 or better. But many of these jobs are just the ones that are being liquidated. In addition, jobs in the North are expanding relatively slowly, and the Negro is in a poor position to compete for many of them. More and more jobs are open only to educated individuals, which means that education is an important key to progress for the Negro in the North. But most Negroes have access primarily to inferior schools, a problem that is in turn tied up with their being for so long restricted to decaying neighborhoods.

These are the salient facts: It is hard for a minority to make significant gains without strong leadership, and one of the historical handicaps of the Negroes is that whenever they have developed a leadership, they have tended to lose it, because of the tendency of many successful Negroes to separate themselves from their original communities. But this may be largely at an end. In the future, we can expect the Negro community to have the advantage of better leadership because of a rising racial consciousness and the fact that major political power can be wielded only by those who succeed in leading the Negro masses.

Second, the white sector of our society is clearly undergoing important changes in attitudes and behavior. Government has begun to act, not only the Federal government but also state and local governments. Churches are becoming actively involved. For the first time the average citizen is forced to face up to the issue of freedom and equality for the Negro.

The ferment goes further. It includes Africa. The fact that large countries in Africa are now run exclusively by Negroes has an impact on both white and Negro in America.

Three steps must be taken now. The first is finally to grant the Negro the rights guaranteed him by the Thirteeenth, Fourteenth, and Fifteenth Amendments. Secondly, we must begin to live in accordance with our democratic faith: we must not continue the discriminating attitudes, prejudices, and irrational behavior patterns that have for so long disturbed his life and ours.

Finally, we must realize that freedom is only the precondition for equality. There remain many poor Negroes and many poor white people in the United States who need jobs and income. A democracy that wants to make intelligent use of its strength, and we possess great strength, must clean up its own deficiencies before it can claim the right to lead the world.

THE ECONOMICS OF THE NEGRO PROBLEM

Charles E. Silberman

Before we can prescribe solutions to the Negro problem, we must understand the nature of that problem. We must recognize first of all that the so-called "Negro revolt" is a fact of life, that it will not disappear until it has accomplished its end. The docile Negro is a figure of the past; in his place stands the revolutionist. Businessmen in particular will find themselves more and more the target of the Negro revolt for several reasons. First, businessmen occupy a strategic position in American society and revolutionists aim their protests at key people.

Second, because poverty and unemployment are major sources of Negro dissatisfaction and unrest, the emphasis in the Negro revolt has already started to shift from civil rights and public accommodations to jobs. In a number of demonstrations in recent months Negroes have been carrying such signs as "I'd like to eat at your lunch counter if I could afford the price of a cup of coffee." Winning the right to eat in restaurants or lunch counters, and to register at hotels, is relatively meaningless to people who are unable to buy the hamburger or the full-course dinner, or pay the cost of the room.

Here are a few facts about the nature of the economic problem affecting Negroes. Two out of three Negro families earn less than $4,000 a year. Negroes account for 10 per cent of the labor force, 20 per cent of total unemployment, 30 per cent of long-term unemployment. Indeed, unemployment is so omnipresent a fact in Negro life that last year only 50 per cent of all Negro men worked steadily at a full-time job. At least half the male labor force was unemployed at some time during the year.

Moreover, the great improvement in the Negro's economic position relative to that of the white population began in World War II, when a shortage of labor opened up a great many jobs that previously had been barred to Negroes, but these opportunities diminished with the slowdown of economic growth after the close of the war. The figures have fluctuated somewhat from year to year but since the war there has been no net improvement in the Negro's relative position vis-a-vis the white's. In fact, the terminal years give a picture of deterioration of median Negro income from 57 per cent of white income in 1952 to 53 per cent in 1962, with slight fluctuations from year to year.

Furthermore, technological change and changes in the structure of the economy are making the problem even more serious. In the years since the end of World War II, for example, 97 per cent of the increase in employment that has occurred in the United States has been in essentially white collar jobs. Yet these are jobs which, because of custom or lack of past training or outright prejudice, Negroes generally do not obtain. Three out of five Negroes hold semiskilled or unskilled blue collar jobs, against three out of ten whites in the same category. Such statistics point to a real unemployment crisis in the Negro community unless some fairly substantial changes are made.

We must next ask why Negroes are in this position. What

are the causes, who is to blame? Are the Negro grievances real or are they simply an example of undue sensitivity?

About five or six weeks ago at the NAM's Congress of American Industry, a Negro businessman gave a speech that created a great deal of enthusiasm among the businessmen present. His speech went something as follows: "Wherever there are people there is progress, and wherever there is progress there are problems. The number one domestic problem in America today is the race problem. It is contrary to the laws of nature for a man to stand still. He must move forward, or the eternal march of progress will push him backward. This the Negro has failed to understand. He believes that the lack of civil rights legislation and the lack of integration have kept him back. But this is not true. His own lack of initiative, courage, integrity, loyalty and wisdom are responsible for his not making the rate of progress that he should make."

This was an interesting speech and the businessmen's reaction was interesting. In a sense, the indictment of American Negroes is correct. Many Negroes do lack ambition, initiative, courage, and wisdom. But this itself should be no comfort to white businessmen or to other white citizens. If these charges are correct, it is because for 350 years we whites have maintained a system in the United States which was designed to destroy ambition and initiative and courage among Negroes, to penalize them for displaying such qualities and, in fact, to prevent the accumulation of wisdom.

We have heard a great deal in recent years about human behavior and what determines it. One of the great lessons of our times derives from the experience of the Nazi concentration camp and the experience of the Red Chinese prisoner-of-war camps during the Korean war. Virtually every study of the impact of the concentration camp has emphasized the fact that in usually a matter of months, sometimes less, mature, independent, highly educated, self-sufficient adults were transformed into fawning, servile, dependent, ambitionless children.

The main pattern of behavior in a concentration camp and in prisoner-of-war camps was servility and a kind of apathy, lack of ambition, and a curious identification with the guards themselves. In Nazi camps some Jewish prisoners of war literally identified with SS guards: if they could get hold of thread and needle, they tried to sew their uniform to make it look a bit more like the SS guards' uniform; they imitated the guard's walk. Under these circumstances the whole personality, character, and behavior of an individual was changed.

Likewise the American Negro for 350 years has been subject to a system designed to destroy ambition, to prevent independence and initiative, and to erode intelligence. Thus if we find that Negroes do not always reflect our goals or manifest the behavior and personality we would like to see, the explanation lies not in their nature but in the character of the society in which we and they have lived.

The first fact is the fact of slavery, which Dr. James Conant has referred to as the congenital defect with which the American republic was born. One cannot understand either the past or the present, our own attitudes, or the attitudes of Negroes without understanding the completely unique character of slavery in the United States. The fact of slavery per se is important but not decisive. Many people have been slaves over the course of history, but the crucial fact here is that the system of slavery that developed in the United States was unique in the history of mankind.

Perhaps the greatest observer of the American character, the Frenchman Alexis de Tocqueville, wrote in 1837 that the only means by which the ancients had maintained slavery were fetters and death. Americans in the South of this country, he wrote, had discovered more intellectual means with which to secure their power. They had employed their despotism and their violence against the human mind. The ancients, de Tocqueville went on to say, had taken great care to prevent the slave from breaking his chains. The Southerners, he said, by contrast had adopted measures to deprive him even of his desire for freedom.

The system of slavery that developed here was utterly different from that which developed in Latin America. There were many reasons for this, but the main one was that Latin America, with its Spanish and Portuguese societies, had, curiously enough, a long tradition of slavery going back many years, a tradition in which enslavement was seen as a catastrophe that might befall any man. As a feudal society in which the Crown had an interest in the souls of all beings, Latin America developed a form of slavery that was essentially contractual, an arrangement in which the master owned the slave's labor but not his soul.

The English colonies in the United States and West Indies faced a totally different problem. Feudalism had ended a long time before. These were societies of free men, so the problem arose of how to justify, how to account for slavery in a society based on contracts between free men. The dilemma was resolved through a belief in the Africans' alleged inferiority. If they were inherently inferior, if they lacked the capacity to be free men, then slavery could be justified and, indeed, defended as a service not only to the masters but to the slaves themselves.

And so a system developed in which slavery was total and absolute. The slave was not a person; he was a piece of property and therefore could not enter into any contract. He could not marry. His wife and children could be sold away. In many states, the law expressly forbade anyone to provide education for slaves, to teach them to read or write. In a number of states, slaves were actually bred for the market.

One result was to destroy any possibility of an independent family organization. Another was to completely emasculate the Negro male. Even the right to defend his marriage bed was denied him. The result was, in short, that this system of slavery, created on the assumption of the Negro's inferiority, produced to a surprising degree the behavior that justified the assumption —just as did the Nazi concentration camp, which so remarkably resembled this system of slavery.

It follows from this that since the Negroes were by then in fact inferior, Americans refused to admit freed Negroes into American society. This was unlike the situation in Latin America, where once the slave became free, there was no difference between his status and that of the white person; Negro bishops served in Brazil as early as the late seventeenth and early eighteenth centuries.

In the United States, the free Negro did not become a member of American society. Most states did not permit Negroes to vote. Many states even in the North denied Negroes the right to jury trial. In the free and open West, four states had laws barring Negroes from entering the states. In 1857 Judge Taney, in the Dred Scott decision, stated that a Negro has no rights a white man need respect.

In the words of the abolitionist Wendell Phillips, emancipation freed the slave but ignored the Negro. It did not admit the Negro to American society. In the South, in particular, the white society insisted on maintaining the pattern of debility and dependency. Indeed, in the Southern system almost any behavior on the part of Negroes was allowed as long as the Negro remained servile and dependent. The one sure way for the Negro to get into trouble was to make some attempt to change his position, which meant that he was "uppity," that he did not "know his place." If a Negro did manage to obtain some education he was well advised to hide the fact. Certainly he should not mention it in the presence of whites.

It would be hard to imagine a system better calculated to destroy ambition, to prevent people from acquiring education than that which existed in the South. Much the same structure evolved in the North. For a time after the Civil War Negroes were hopeful of entering American society, but then, fairly rapidly, their so-called "friends" lost interest in the problem of the Negro. Curiously enough, the whole system of Jim Crow, the whole system of segregation, which Southerners insist cannot be changed rapidly because customs do not change rapidly, was a late innovation. From the end of the Civil War until the middle 1890s, segregation did not exist in the South.

Until 1890, segregation was not ensconced except possibly in railroad transportation. But the dam broke in the late 1890s and early 1900s, when the whole system of legal segregation that is now defended as the old Southern tradition was established. One interesting measure of the change is that in 1896 there were 130,334 registered Negro voters in the state of Louisiana. By 1904, there were 1,342. With such speed was the structure established.

The system of segregation was extended to the North in the beginning of the century. After the Civil War in New York City, for example, Negroes had been permitted to go anywhere. In the early 1900s a Negro YMCA was built. At that point Negroes were barred from all other YMCAs and were refused admission to theatres, restaurants, and so on.

Woodrow Wilson, elected President in 1912, had campaigned on the New Freedom, but after his inauguration he imposed a system of segregation in Federal offices where there had been no segregation. Negroes were barred from using the restaurants and washrooms they had been using for thirty to forty years.

Even today white people quite unconsciously treat Negroes as children. Whether unconscious or not, however, such behavior is patronizing and condescending. One calls a Negro "boy," a term that reflects the unconscious subordination of Negro to white. We have a concept of place: we do not consciously discriminate against Negroes in employment, perhaps, but we have a notion of appropriate and inappropriate jobs. During a survey made across the country of the way in which companies were complying with the *Plans for Progress,* one firm, when asked whether it had any Negro salesmen, replied, "Why would we have Negro salesmen when we don't have any Negro customers?" One hires a Negro salesman to sell only to Negroes. Yet this is not a concept we apply to the various ethnic groups among the white population.

We have developed, in our relations with Negroes, a pattern and tradition of manipulation. Consider, for example, the group of Oakland businessmen who tried to develop a program to increase Negro employment. They wanted to meet with a group of Negroes to discuss the program, but they did not want "any of those agitators from the NAACP." Consequently, a committee was assembled of men who would not argue, who would be very agreeable. The only problem was they did not represent the Negro community. And before long, the community exploded in anger over the program. For this tradition of patronization and manipulation—superior-inferior, however it is described— is now arousing an enormous anger that has been suppressed for generations. Many stories are told about an old and valued Negro employee, or the son of such an employee, who suddenly expresses anger or hatred after having been apparently happy for twenty or thirty years. The anger is not new. What is new is simply that Negroes now feel safe, feel free to express the anger.

As James Baldwin has put it, to be a Negro in this country and to be relatively conscious is to be enraged all or most all of the time. The anger may sometimes result in irrational or what seems to be irrational behavior. One can simply say that the response to 350 years of exclusion from American society is not likely to be sweet reasonableness.

We can expect to encounter anger, hatred, unreasonableness— these are simply facts of life.

Lastly, the grievances are very real. The reasons for the economic plight of the Negroes lie very deep in the history of the Negro in the United States, and if blame is to be assessed, the blame will have to be placed on white society. It is not so important where the blame is placed, however, as where the responsibility is placed, and the responsibility, it seems to me, belongs to the white population that has maintained, frequently unconsciously, frequently consciously, a society that has excluded the Negro for 350 years.

The basic approach that Negroes are taking to redress their grievances is political—the use of power. It is perfectly plausible that this should solve the problem. Since they were denied a place in American society because of their group membership, Negroes should inevitably demand admission because of their group membership. And when the editorial writers of the *New York Times* wax righteous over the violation of the American dream of judging individuals by their performance as individuals, instead of as members of a group, they must be reminded that we haven't been dealing with Negroes on this basis.

Every other ethnic group has made its way up into middle class through group pressure, through political activity, through the use of power. We tend to deny this because, ideologically, American politics stresses the importance of the individual, but the fact remains that every political ticket that is ever put together is balanced in terms of group membership. This has been the means to political power, and it is a little late in the history of the United States suddenly to change the rules and say to the Negro, Although other groups have helped themselves by group activity, you must make it on your own as individuals.

This means that there are going to be demands for quotas, for preferential treatment. These are simply necessary and inevitable tactics. The only test of change lies in numbers; this is the meaning of a demand for a quota. No business can determine the "right" number of Negroes it should employ; but unless there is some discussion of numbers, the result of accepting the principle of nondiscrimination tends to be in practice simply the hiring of one or two Negroes for show. Dick Gregory has a new joke about walking down the street and seeing a big sign advertising Hertz-Rent-a-Negro.

Tactics will vary according to the kind of power used. They will include boycotts, demonstrations, picketing, sit-ins, and direct action of this sort. They will involve much more subtle weapons, such as analysis of investment portfolios. Negro pressure on the city administration in New York, for example, has led the city to seek a change in the state law so that trustees of the municipal pension fund can withdraw investments from companies that discriminate against Negroes, and limit their investments to companies which do not discriminate. Tactics will vary all the way from this kind of security analysis technique to the most direct use of physical force, where individuals simply come into a plant and sit in to block activity.

Let me conclude by pointing out that businessmen generally think of themselves as conservatives. They have a chance now to act truly as conservatives, to conserve American society by changing what has to be changed, by modifying what has to be modified, by innovating where innovation is necessary.

Unless these changes are made, we will have some very difficult years. Business today has an enormous opportunity. The delays and outright resistance to law in the South—ten years after the Supreme Court decision on school desegration less than 1 per cent of the Negro school children in the South are attending desegregated schools—have destroyed the Negroes' faith in white integrity and in the integrity of the judicial process. If businessmen act on their own, not simply in response to pressures to create job opportunities for Negroes, they will be taking advantage of a golden opportunity to restore at least some portion of that lost faith in white integrity and in the possibility of the American system's working for the Negro as well as the white.

JOBS AND INCOME

Whitney Young

I will preface this presentation with one or two assumptions. First, I assume that you want me to speak with as much candor as possible. I am not here to entertain or falsely reassure you. Some years ago, the business community simply wanted to be entertained in its discussion about Negroes; they asked for information from their maids or from other Negroes who they thought would say the things they wanted to hear.

I thought this era was over until the industrialist to whom Mr. Silberman referred was asked to address one of the national trade groups. Then we had to start all over again, saying, "See, here we are again, the white community is still trying to fool itself—it still does not take the Negro seriously. It seeks out the facts it wants to hear." Of course any group has the right to invite any speaker it wants, but this kind of approach will not influence a single Negro. Such a speaker will not influence even his own employees after working hours—in spite of the fact that he has made a million dollars selling cosmetics to "irresponsible" Negroes. Effective selling does not make him a competent social scientist; it makes him a competent businessman.

We have to think seriously not so much about exposing the businessmen but about exposing the Negro community at a moment of conflict to the fact that the business community is still engaged in this kind of game. Invite a successful industrialist in the cosmetic field if you want to be entertained, but do not invite him if you want serious consideration of the problem of race relations in this country.

My next assumption is that we all recognize the historical inequities that Mr. Silberman has outlined so well. We are not talking about a mild inconvenience for Negroes, nor a recession, nor even a depression—we are describing a catastrophe, a disaster that is fast becoming a national disgrace. The Negro is really hurt. He is not seeking just social acceptance and status and prestige.

Third, I assume that American business, when it makes up its mind to do something, has the ability, the know-how, the genius, the creativity to do what it wants to do. We saw this in the beginning of World War II with the sudden conversion of peacetime industry to the making of airplanes. The reason the problem of the Negro in industry has not been solved up to now is that the business community did not really make up its mind until the last year or so to do something about it.

If this decision has truly been made, I am confident that change is possible. Of course, if the community does not intend to fulfill its promises, excuses are always available: there are no Negroes qualified; or the Negro does not apply for the position. One can always find a reason not to do something. But I would charge you to spend your time trying to determine how you can do this rather than why you cannot. Then a change will take place.

The year 1963, the year of the Negro revolution and of a

summer of discontent, taught us many things. It taught the Urban League and Negro leadership in general that we can no longer generalize about the problem of race relations. We can no longer assign nice clean categories and classifications to groups, institutions, and sections of the country. We can no longer say that business is biased and conservative or that labor is liberal and free of prejudice, that the South has a monopoly on all the bigots, and the North on all liberals. Or that Negroes have a monopoly on morality, and white people on evil.

We found this year some bigots in the North who were as sophisticated and brutal as any we ever grew in the South. We have found in labor, especially in the building trades, some bigots as big as we ever found among management. We have found that Negroes also have learned well how to be demagogues and how to exploit poverty and misery. And conversely, we have found, not enough, but we have found people in the South with real understanding of the problem and real conviction about its solution; we have found among business people and among white people generally, some individuals and groups of real conviction.

From this point on we must look at individuals and not generalize about sections of the country or business per se, or labor per se. It also seems quite clear that business has an obvious stake in resolving this problem, for while it cannot function in the harmful climate of conflict, tension, and discord, it can see in the Negro population a whole reservoir of potential producers and consumers.

Most important, if the free enterprise system, which could produce all the nation's annual consumer needs in about three months if it wanted to, is at all concerned about winning favor around the world, it must understand that the Negro is the barometer of the effectiveness of the free enterprise system. Seventy-five per cent of the world's population happens to be nonwhite. If in the free enterprise system the Negro is disproportionately unemployed, if he is low man on the totem pole, if he gets all the responsibilities and none of the rewards of the system, then the system is not likely to attract those countries of the world who are now shopping around for the system that will work best for them. The real test of an economic system is not the extent to which it gives to those who have, but the extent to which it gives more to those who have not. In this sense, what happens to the Negro vis-a-vis American business is the crucial test.

We have also reached the point where we can no longer pick out a single facet of this problem, a facet that often lies conveniently beyond our own area of responsibility. Thus the businessman will say the problem is education. The educator will say the problem is housing. When I talk to employers about employing Negroes, they say, "You know, Mr. Young, if the Negro were better trained, better educated, or more skilled, we would employ him." And I say, "Well, this makes sense," and off I go to see the educator. And the educator says to me, "Well, Mr. Young, the problem is housing. The Negroes' family life does not permit them to buy encyclopedias and hear intelligent dialogue; they are overcrowded; three and four in a room does not make an environment conducive to study and therefore cultural gaps are created."

So I say, "Well, this makes sense; we could change the housing pattern." And I go to see the real estate men and the builders and they say, "We'll be happy to build houses for Negroes providing they have money." And I am back with the employer. This is the vicious circle, and one cannot intervene more effectively at one point than at another.

All this may be satisfying to your conscience, but it is not facing up to the facts of life. You do have a stake not just in hiring Negroes but in seeing that they receive an adequate education, that they can obtain adequate housing. To ignore the facts is to be naïve.

I have said to several business groups that the Negro and the businessman have a great deal in common in addition to the common stake I have mentioned. Both have been victims of a stereotype. You can recall in the years before the cartoonist became a businessman how he used to characterize the American businessman: with dollar signs for eyeballs and an adding machine for a brain, the businessman emerged as the personally insensitive, socially irresponsible, esthetically illiterate fat man who saw other people only as impersonal cogs in a vast industrial machine.

The Negro has also suffered from a stereotyped characterization: he has been pictured as lazy, happy-go-lucky, and simpleminded; uncomfortable in a house with more than three rooms; incapable of mastering complicated data and technical information; addicted to fun on Saturday nights.

Businessmen have almost removed their stereotype from the public mind. They have removed it because it was a stereotype and not a statement of fact. But businessmen themselves have also changed; increasingly, they have shown, not completely in the area of race relations yet but in other areas, a sense of social responsibility. Academic training has helped them see people as more than impersonal cogs in a machine. And of course their image has been improved by the work of good public relations men.

Now I would like to see an attempt to change the Negro stereotype. Enough Negroes have achieved success and made great contributions to the country to indicate that the Negro is not a simple-minded, happy-go-lucky, lazy individual, and that, in fact, he'd like to have fun on Monday and Tuesday nights as well as on Saturday nights.

Time alone will never solve any problem, and wishful thinking will not change a thing. People change things. And while 100 years may be a short time in history it is a long time in the life of a human being. Even two or three generations may be a long time if you are a Negro, because Negroes do not live as long as whites. It is certainly a long time in the life of a parent who is trying to bring up his child with the concept of democracy we all want to believe.

I think we have to understand also that it is unfair to engage in the rather common practice of comparing the Negroes' situation with the situation that confronted other minority groups who come to this country—the Irish, the Italians, the Jews, who through perseverance, hard work, and diligence managed to acquire skills and money and to escape a life of poverty. This comparison is not sound. The Negro is unique. He was the only involuntary migrant. No other group in the history of mankind ever faced what the Negro has faced. No other group in history ever experienced a conscious effort made by others to strip it of the basic institution of the family. At the time when Negroes were taken from Africa, husband and wife were never brought together. After they got to this country, and were sold every six months or every year on the block, husband and wife were never sold together, and almost without exception the mother was separated from the children. During this period, there was a premium put on promiscuity; the more reproduction, the more slaves. Up to 100 years ago, when the Emancipation Proclamation was signed, and even after that point, there was an attempt to humiliate and keep the Negro male in such a situation that revolt would be difficult. This was no accident; it was consciously, deliberately done.

It was done because it was recognized that if you want to keep a group weak and disorganized you weaken its basic institution, the family. No other group has ever faced this. The Jew, the Italian, the Irish faced an entirely different situation. Of the people who came here, many had skills, many had families to receive them. They came in families or they sent back and got their families. With the Negro this did not happen.

The other unique factor is that the Negro, once here, even if he somehow acquired a sufficient amount of affluence to escape, could not escape because of his color. Members of religious or national groups can change their affiliations and then even run for president. They can change and get lost in the larger society. But color has a note of finality; the Negro is unable to get lost. In fact, only in recent years in the North has the Negro been able to break out of the ghetto, which formerly entrapped him despite the money he might have had. This was possible only because of the passage of new laws.

For these reasons, the National Urban League, in a what-do-you-do situation, composed the domestic Marshall Plan last year. Some of the aspects of the plan have been distorted. People have called it preferential treatment. In Chicago a group whom I addressed called it compensatory activity; in Cleveland, they called it affirmative action; in Miami, they were rather cautious and called it a plan to do good.

But whatever title you give it, the basic idea is that at this point, given the history of 300 years of denial, of minimum opportunities for education, economic affluence, and cultural growth, given the gap that now exists, it is impossible to bring about significant change in the foreseeable future by a simple declaration. We cannot ignore the past, because the past exists in the present. And the scales of justice have been so heavily weighted against the Negro that they cannot now be balanced simply by adding equal weights.

A human being who has been undernourished, who has not had enough vitamins, cannot be made equal to a well-nourished human being simply by being given now an equal amount of food. He must be built up for a brief period before equal opportunity will have any meaning at all. I want to emphasize the word "brief": we are not asking for equal time, we are not asking for 300 years of preferential treatment, but we are asking for unequal inputs for a brief period.

An anemic individual needs a blood transfusion if he is going to compete with another human being who is not anemic. I have used the comparison of two men running a mile race—one running in track shoes on a cinder track, the other barefooted in sand. And at the half-way point, there is a Supreme Court decision or an executive order, or a threat of a boycott. This race, it is decided, is not quite fair. So they put the Negro in track shoes and on the cinder track. One second later, somebody says,

"I don't know why you are behind. You must be inferior." Well, the Negro is behind because he has already been handicapped— he has been running in sand barefooted while the other man has been on a cinder track.

If we are to do more than engage in academic verbalizing or conscience salving, we must admit this and move on to some deliberate effort. The Marshall Plan goes beyond employment: it aims at a saturation of resources, of personnel, and of materials in a community that needs it most. We need education, we need health and welfare facilities.

In the past Negroes have been taught and counselled by the most inferior personnel; they have had access to the most inferior facilities in a low economic area. We are saying today that this is where the best teachers must be, where the best social workers must be, and we do not think this is a radical concept. Medicine has been doing it all along. Had medicine been doing what education and social work have been doing all these years, internes would be performing complicated surgery while skilled surgeons were treating the common cold. That is actually what we have been doing in education and in social work.

We are saying that in employment it is not enough simply to put up a sign stating that you are a fair-employment company, or to autograph the President's *Plans for Progress*, or to put an ad in the newspaper. Today you must make a conscious effort—you must reach out. You must aggressively recruit through the organizations, the schools, the counsellors. You must also look at your own personnel and see whether some one there with a college degree has been pushing a broom.

We are suggesting that you make this a special effort, and a realistic one. Many plants after much soul searching decide to hire Negroes. They get in touch with us, but what they want are people like Ralph Bunche for accountants or Lena Horne typing 100 words a minute as a secretary. Now while we may have a few people of this caliber because of the limited job opportunities for Negroes, we run out of Lena Hornes and Ralph Bunches pretty fast. But we know that you have some jobs for ordinary, even dumb, white people, and we want some of those jobs too. We have some ordinary dumb Negroes, and we need jobs all up and down—for the whole group.

Let us look at the important problem of screening and testing. As I have said, if you don't want to hire Negroes, you can always get out of it. But if you want to, you can. You must, however, use realistic devices and tools and not tests that are designed to exclude the Negro.

The Marshall Plan does not make suggestions to white people alone. It also outlines the role of Negroes, particularly middle class Negroes, who should make a special effort to help. When we talk about marches—the march on Washington, marches in front of the 5 and 10 cent store and the courthouse, marches of children to the library, marches of parents to PTA meetings, to adult training centers, to retraining centers, to policy making bodies—we assume that the Negro who has achieved a measure of success has the responsibility for helping others. The whole burden does not lie squarely on white people; we are sharing it with them.

The Urban League has tried to lead the way in showing what can be done. Our secretarial program is a good example of what can be done for people who do not quite measure up to necessary standards. In this program, we recruited forty girls for our first class from the rolls of the Civil Service and from groups who had rejected the girls' applications. All the girls had completed courses in secretarial schools or business schools, or they had taken typing in high school. But they fell just a little short. As a result they seemed destined to be domestic workers or little better. We gave these girls an eleven-week refresher orientation course in which we did more than help them with the technical skills; we told them about the tests they would have to take and we tried to help them get rid of some of the anxiety and hopelessness they had felt when they first applied.

We also told them about such things as grooming. At the end of the course this group of forty girls not only came up to the passing level but went far beyond it. And the six or seven companies that contributed to this project and participated in it by sending their secretaries and their business people down to talk to the girls were waiting outside the door to hire them.

This was the program we worked out with New York University and their School of Business. And what we have done, business can do. Business ought to take a second and more sympathetic look at the people they have been turning down. We are as concerned now, you see, about the depth of your feeling as we are about the depth of your interview. With a little more heart and understanding, and a little more awareness of the dynamics of the interview and testing processes, you can salvage some excellent employees.

In Chicago the Urban League worked out a retraining plan with the Yellow Cab Company and Shell Oil in conjunction with the Public Welfare Department. In three months, 200 Negro men were trained to become taxicab drivers and service station attendants. This means not only that 200 men are off the relief rolls and making $100 a week but also that their role in their families—their role as parents—has changed. Again, this is a drop in the bucket, but it is an illustration of what can be done if one really sets out to do it.

The Urban League is just one of a number of organizations in the field. We have worked out a way of communicating with other responsible groups, such as CORE, NAACP, ministers' groups in some cities, and the student protest movement, and we have set up certain divisions of labor and deployed certain of our personnel, according to our philosophy, our history and the training of our staff.

It is important that business itself not try to identify a Negro leader but that it recognize and work with the established leadership that Negroes themselves have identified, whether the business community considers that leadership sufficiently responsible

or not. Moreover, business should recognize the limits of what
the Urban League can do: the League can help find responsible
Negroes; it can communicate to others in the community what
a company's policies really are; it can work out some of the
problems that may come up. But the Urban League is not in
the painting business—it cannot make a segregated company look
integrated, nor does it intend to help companies discriminate
with more sophistication, or segregate with more subtlety.

We can help you intelligently to integrate your company.
Twenty years ago the Urban League advised business to integrate, and those very few companies that did integrate have
not been bothered by threats of boycotts. The protests and
revolt organizations would not exist today had business in general moved more aggressively in past years. Such organizations
become necessary and powerful to the extent that there is a
need for them. If there is no need, they do not exist. And if
you are concerned now about their getting too powerful, you
must blame the business community, which failed to work with
the group whose methods were persuasion and negotiation. But
it is not too late. There are always people who are more concerned about the one or two irresponsible acts that have occurred during this revolution than about the underlying cause.
Any revolution is bound to have its irresponsible protagonists.
Indeed, when one remembers the provocation, the long history
of abuse, and the anger that seethes now in Negro communities
we have been very fortunate to have so few incidents. Most of
the other organizations operate with volunteers, whose motives
often differ from those of a professional staff. In one case, for
example, a group dumped garbage in front of City Hall. This
was bad and none of us approved of it, but I also remember
that during the war there was a soldier in my company in
Europe who wanted to take a hand grenade and destroy the
whole German army. There is always an irresponsible element.

The leadership has tried to keep this to a minimum. But the
question of whether the responsible leadership will be able to

retain its position is a question we cannot answer; it is a question you can answer. A leadership retains its position if it wins some victories, if it pays off in a tangible way, if there is a responsible response from the leadership of the white community. If there is no response, or very little tangible response, then our position will be weakened if not destroyed. And the next march on Washington will not be led by Whitney Young and Roy Wilkins *and* Jim Farmer. For if you think Jim Farmer is radical, you ought to see some of the people standing in the wings, ready to take over.

In the light of their motives and provocations, Negroes last year showed a kind of responsible restraint that the whole society ought to be able to appreciate. Now it is your turn. This is your year. Last year was the year of confrontation. All Americans were faced with the fact of the Negro revolt. This is the year of decision making, the year for the business community, the congressmen, the legislators, and everybody else to be responsible.

If this happens, then the radicals who would have us truly be revolutionaries will not be able to take over; we will have shown that we can win in this manner. From here on, I think we will have a different kind of struggle than we have had in the past. It is no longer a conflict between good and bad, between white and black; it is now a struggle between intelligent, decent people who care, and callous, cruel people who are completely indifferent to this problem.

There is more white support for this struggle today than ever before. And we are not concerned about the so-called "hardening" of attitudes—a Negro mother living with her five children in a two-room tenement house, where the rats are biting her kids, couldn't care less about the hardening attitudes of some white persons. Negroes know that until 1962-1963 about 10 per cent of the white population in this country wanted integration; about 10 per cent were hostile to it and were fighting actively against it; and the other eighty per cent were largely ignoring the whole issue.

Today nobody is ignoring it. Some of that middle band have moved to the hostile side; nevertheless, 70 to 75 per cent of the people in the country are willing to help integration succeed. This of course does not imply intermarriage or living next door to derelicts. Any Negro who can afford to move to the suburbs must have as much education and as much ability as any white person who lives in that neighborhood. If a Negro can afford the suburbs it is not because he is a prosperous businessman, as some of his white neighbors might be, but because he is probably a doctor or a lawyer or a member of some other profession. His white neighbors, in some cases, qualified for residency simply by having had enough money. Perhaps they were in real estate or some other type of business that the Negro can never enter. But have no fear, the Negro numbers man won't move out there because he has to stay with his business in Harlem.

I do have confidence that change is going to take place. It is going to take place not because institutions as such will move but because individual companies with leadership, secure businessmen, will move, will see their stake in the problem and their role. But I am ever mindful of the fact that Negroes were not welcomed in baseball because there suddenly appeared a nice, well-scrubbed Negro who had a college degree and a lot of ability. That is not why Negroes are now a part of professional baseball. They are there today not because of Jackie Robinson but because of Branch Rickey, a man who had the courage to stand up and say, "No. I am tired of living a lie. I am going to make this a normal American game."

Now we need some Branch Rickeys in other places. We need them in business. We need them in education. We need them in the building business. Maybe we will even find them one day in the churches. But we do need them. You can be a Branch Rickey. There are people right in this room who could revolutionize the pattern of today. I am confident that change will take place, and the fact that you are here is an indication that you are eager to make a start.

WHITE-NEGRO CONFRONTATIONS

Thomas Pettigrew

This presentation will attempt to shift our discussion from global social analysis to a psychological analysis of what current events mean particularly to the Negro community.

I will begin with a story about one of my favorite professors, the late Professor Samuel Stouffer, who was one of America's greatest sociologists. Stouffer used to become incensed when, after he had given an absolutely magnificent fifty-minute lecture in which he presented some of his latest findings, particularly data from public opinion polls, a Harvard undergraduate would come up and say, "Dr. Stouffer, who didn't know that? Did you spend all that money just to find that out?" Stouffer retaliated by devising what can be called a "conventional wisdom" test, in which the answers to the questions were true according to conventional wisdom but false according to the findings of vigorous social research.

He handed out the questionnaire to each of his undergraduate classes. The great majority, 89 per cent of the students, missed every single item. The moral is clear—behavioral science findings generally look obvious only after the fact, not necessarily before. Stouffer's favorite item in that test, which almost always succeeded in catching the undergraduates, concerned the Air Corps and Military Police and their morale in World War II. Briefly, the Air Corps had a system of very rapid advancement in World War II. It was possible to go from second lieutenant to colonel in a few years, and many did as a matter of fact. In the Military Police, one was lucky to attain the rank of corporal after 2½ years.

Now conventional wisdom would expect those in the Military Police to be extremely frustrated with this slow rate of progress and those in the Air Corps to have a high level of morale because of the rate of their promotions. As a matter of fact, it was exactly the opposite. Those in the Air Corps were extremely frustrated and upset over the issue of promotion while those in the Military Police were relatively satisfied. Conventional wisdom would be off in its judgment because it would have failed, as it often does, to take into account how the people in the situation view it themselves. In the Air Corps, for example, the men compared their own promotions with those of others around them. If, for instance, a man rose from second lieutenant to major he would feel discriminated against if his buddy from pilot school became a colonel. But in the Military Police, one could look around and see that others were only corporals, too; this made everyone relatively satisfied.

One of the principles we seem to have demonstrated in the last twenty years in social science is what we call the theory of relative deprivation. When we talk about social motivation, we are not talking of hunger, thirst, or the other basic physiological drives, but what an individual has, not in absolute terms, but in relation to what he aspires to. It refers to what he realistically and rightfully expects to attain.

To bring the analogy into the subject of the current Negro revolution, the Negro was angry and frustrated for many years, but his case was analogous to the Military Police. He did not like his slow promotion, his slow gains in America, but he had never known anything else. Today, the new Negro, as he is called, is analogous to the Air Corps in World War II. His aspiration levels have risen very rapidly. In fact, his progress of the last twenty years has caused his aspiration level to go up much faster than his actual gains, even though in some cases these have been dramatic.

Thus after twenty years of progress, particularly in certain areas, the Negro is nevertheless considerably more frustrated today than he was at the beginning of this period of change because, while his absolute standard has been going up, his aspiration level has been rising much faster. His relative deprivation, the difference between what he has and what he expects to have, and what he thinks is his right to have, is now probably greater than at any other time in American history.

Let us first take up the actual gains that have been made and compare these to the psychological losses that Negro Americans are operating under today. First, the urban concentration of Negroes has continued to increase from 1940 to 1960. The percentage, not just the absolute number, of Negroes living in New York and Philadelphia has more than doubled, and in Chicago, Los Angeles, and Detroit it has tripled. And these are our five largest cities. The Negro does not come to just the city, he comes to the largest cities. By 1960, the Negro was more urban than the white population and was concentrated in the largest metropolitan areas. More than half of all Negroes live in cities of more than half a million people.

There are several implications of this massive movement that should be underlined. First, the Negro has been moving from the areas most resistant to racial change—the rural South—to those that are least resistant. Second, this urban concentration leads to sophistication. It makes people cognizant of exactly what it is that discrimination denies them. Back on the farm in the South the Negro is not nearly so aware of what he is missing. Third, it produces large concentrations of Negroes, which improves communications and makes possible the formation of protest organizations that cannot be established in rural areas. And fourth, it enables Negroes to benefit in part, but only in part, from the higher standard of living in cities.

The gains made in the last twenty to twenty-five years by Negro Americans are largely attributable to the Negro's own initiative in coming to the city, and not to a decrease in formal discrimination. Formal discrimination has decreased during these twenty years, but this accounts for only a small part of the progress. The biggest gains have derived simply from the fact that the Negro moved from a poor to a wealthier area.

Of the gains, the first is health. From 1900 to 1960, the Negro American's life expectancy at birth increased twice as fast as that of the white population. At the turn of the century the average Negro lived thirty-five years. Today, the life expectancy of the average Negro, which varies a little by sex, is about sixty-five years. This is a tremendous difference. From 1950 to 1960, using age-adjusted mortality rates, Negro life expectancy actually improved as much as it did from 1900 to 1950.

In employment, from 1950 to 1960, the Negroes made more of a percentage improvement than did white workers. Of course, the Negro had such a low base that a little employment increase might make a substantial percentage increase. In government, since the beginning of the Kennedy administration, Negro employment in the more responsible jobs has increased even more rapidly than in less responsible jobs, owing largely to the government's crash program of the last three years in upgrading Negroes.

In business, since 1947 Negro savings and loan associations have increased their assets thirty-two times. Over-all, the savings and loan associations in the United States have increased their assets in that same period three times.

Negro commercial banks have increased their assets from 5 million to 53 million dollars since 1940, while commercial banks in general have increased their assets over five times.

Negro-controlled insurance companies have doubled their assets since 1951 and now have at least 320 million dollars.

Individual income for Negroes went up 54 per cent from 1950 to 1960; for families it went up 73 per cent. In 1961, 20 per cent of all Negro families made more than $6,000, as compared to 4 per cent in 1945.

The percentage of Negro Americans living in standard housing, as compared with census-defined substandard housing, doubled from 1950 to 1960.

In politics, over a million more Negroes voted in 1962 than did in 1950. The fact is often overlooked, particularly by Goldwater people who seem to count the Southern states as if they were in their hip pocket, that the Negro not only made the difference in the crucial swing of industrial states New York and Pennsylvania for President Kennedy in 1960 but he also made much more of the difference in North Carolina, South Carolina, Georgia, and Texas. This pattern will increase, not decrease. Moreover, the Negro is actually getting to be a determinant of the electoral vote in many Southern states.

In education, from 1940 to 1960 the percentage of Negroes attending college more than doubled. A particularly crucial group in hiring is the twenty-five to twenty-nine-year-old group, chosen by the census presumably because they have finished their formal education. The median number of years of education achieved by Negroes in this age group in 1940 was seven. By 1959 the median number for this same age group had risen to eleven years, which is one year short of a high school graduation. And four years is a phenomenal difference in education.

All these gains have led directly to an enormous rise in Negro aspirations, a rise that had became noteworthy by the 1950s. In 1954, Stouffer again did a poll, this time on McCarthyism and the effect of McCarthyism on American public opinion. It was the biggest, most expensive, best-done poll in the history of polling in the United States, and it happened to be done in a rather significant month, May 1954, just when the Supreme Court's school desegregation opinion was published. Stouffer's first question was, "Do you think life will be better for you in the next five years? Better than it is now, or was, or do you think it will be about the same?" I have recently analyzed the data collected from Negroes, which was sorted by region, education, employment and so forth. Any way the data are considered, in 1954 a much higher proportion of Negroes than whites said that they believed life was going to be better for them in the next five years. The increase in their aspirations had clearly started by 1954.

One might say that after all 1954 was a vintage year, and the polls were taken at just the time when the aspiration level was up. According to the polls since 1954, however, the aspiration level for Negroes has continued and is continuing to go up.

The most recent evidence on this is the 1963 Louis Harris poll, which indicated that 73 per cent of the Negroes in the United States believe that the attitude of the whites will improve in the next five years; 63 per cent believe that whites will accept racial change without violence; 85 per cent of those who do not own their homes now desire to own a home and think that they will; and 30 per cent of those not now in white collar employment believe that they are qualified for white collar employment.

Mixed up in this is an exalted, almost a pathetic, faith in education. This gets overlooked during discussions of the higher drop-out rates among Negroes than among whites. There are reasons for this high drop-out rate among Negroes; many have been enumerated already in this conference. But the drop-out rate does not mean that Negroes do not aspire to education—they do. When occupation, background, and other variables are controlled, Negroes have much greater faith in education than do whites.

This faith is rooted in the reconstruction education that

Abolitionist school marms pumped into the South right after the Civil War. As Booker T. Washington reflected, it implies a belief that the education of Negroes will in time break down racial barriers. To some extent this is still believed. One in five of the Negro respondents in the Harris poll had a child who had dropped out of school before finishing high school. Nevertheless, 97 per cent of the sample wanted their children to finish high school and were very sorry if they had not been able to.

Another study found that 83 per cent of Negro mothers in the Northeast intended that their sons go to college, though frequently these mothers had no idea, and no way of finding out, how one gets to college. How to take the right college preparatory course and get the forms to apply—knowledge of these simple preliminaries, which middle class whites, and for that matter, middle class Negroes, know all about, is not common knowledge for the lower class Negro. It is difficult for him to get such information and carry through on this faith. But the faith is there and can be utilized, and this makes the problem of retraining a little easier.

Notice that all these gains by Negroes were gains made over their previous conditions and not gains made in relationship to the present white status. Compared to white standards, the picture becomes a very different one. As Whitney Young has implied, the Negro is on a treadmill and really stands to lose in the coming years, at least in relative terms; just holding his own will be a problem.

Thus if we compare the current status of Negro Americans with the current status of middle class whites, the relative deprivation of the Negro comes into effect with great force, and actual gains start translating themselves immediately into psychological war.

Let us consider from this point of view each of the areas of gain we have just reviewed. There are still substantial segments of the Negro population in the Black Belt section. We forget they are there because of the heavy trend in urbanization, but they are there—millions of them, who for the most part cannot vote. In health, the life expectancy of Negro Americans has risen dramatically, but it still lies six to eight years behind that of the white population. To put this in more human terms, the percentage of young widows of fifty-four years or younger in the Negro community is double that of the number in the white community. This is a reflection of the six- to eight-year difference in life expectancy between the Negro and the white male.

In employment, since 1950, most unionized industries have maintained their employment policies with regard to race—we have had a decade without any significant changes or improvements. The rate of unemployment among Negro youth has been almost twice the rate among white youth. There were gains of sorts in employment in the 1950-1960 decade, but if the same rate of gain were to continue into the future, Negroes would not be proportionately represented among clerical workers until 1992 and they would not have proportional representation among skilled workers until the fifth year of the next century. They would not have proportional representation among professionals until the seventeenth year of the next century, or among sales workers until 2114, or among business managers and proprietors until 2730, which is eight centuries away.

One of the reasons for their failure to gain in the business, managerial, and proprietary areas is discrimination at the executive level. And since Negro business is miniscule, it cannot absorb many more managers.

We have noted that the assets of savings banks have increased thirty-two times. Even with that increase, however, total assets in Negro savings and loans constitute only 3/10 of 1 per cent of the total assets of all savings and loans institutions.

In insurance companies, if the assets of all fifty-five Negro-controlled insurance companies were combined, they would equal better than 320 million dollars, but this is only a very small fraction of the assets of any one of the larger insurance companies in the United States.

Income represents the most disappointing psychological loss of all. The median Negro family income did not change in the fifties; it hit its high point right after the Korean War and since then has moved downward. The median family income still remains at about 50 per cent of the median family income among the white population. Average family income is even less. In the South, median Negro family income is 40 per cent of that of the white population. The difference in dollars is widening rapidly even when the ratio remains the same.

In spite of vast differences in adequacy of housing, the Negroes in Chicago pay the same median rent as do whites in Chicago. The existence of the two separate housing markets has not changed. In fact, during the forties the separation became more pronounced. Residential segregation increased in every standard metropolitan area of the United States. In the fifties the national level remained the same, though there were different patterns in different cities. Some cities actually turned the corner in the fifties and began to slowly come back to a somewhat less segregated residential pattern. Many cities continued the trend of the forties and the over-all trend remains the same.

In the political arena, denial of franchise in the Black Belt is still rigidly enforced. Education is inferior; it is inferior in Harlem schools with all Negroes and in the so-called "Negro colleges" in the South. Segregationists seem to feel that the Negro wants integrated education because he wants to be like a white man, he wants to enter a white world. But the major motivation actually derives not from the fact that the Negro wants to be like whites but from the fact that he knows he will not get a decent education unless he is in a school with whites. It is a simple political factor of American life.

We have seen that the percentage of Negroes in college doubled from 1940 to 1960. This percentage in 1960, however, was still only about half that of whites.

We have heard that the buying power of Negro Americans is greater than the buying power of Canadians—there are approximately 18 or 19 million people in each group—and we have heard that the percentage of Negroes who go to college is almost double the percentage in the British Isles. We have heard that the nonwhites in the West have an income equal to the whites in the South. All these statements, at least from a social-psychological point of view, are irrelevant. Psychologically the Negro does not compare his buying power with that of the Canadians; he does not compare his college admission to that in the British Isles. On the West Coast he does not compare his income to that of a white Southerner; he compares it to that of a white Westerner.

The Negro American judges himself in the only cultural terms he knows—those of the United States and its so-called "people of plenty." For fourteen generations he has been an American. He has no other terms by which to judge himself. That is why the principle of relative deprivation becomes the primary dynamic behind the Negro protest today.

One more factor is the psychological effect of emerging Africa on Negro Americans. Recent polls indicate a very interesting dual effect of newly independent countries in Africa on Negro Americans. On the one hand, Negro Americans are proud of these countries, and they are pleased to see the head of state of Nigeria come to Washington and be greeted with pomp and ceremony by the President of the United States, or to see black delegates to the UN wooed by the United States because we need their votes in Assembly. This is all very ego-enhancing.

On the other hand it has a relatively depriving aspect too. Until recently a Negro American had the most prestige and was the most respected black man in the world. No matter how lowly his position within the United States, he was the most Western and materially the best off of all black people. Today, when an African visitor comes to the United States, he says to the Negro rather bluntly and repeatedly, "Yes, yes, you still are materially better off. You have a car; I don't own a car yet. But I am free." And that cuts in a very special way.

The third relatively depriving factor that is operating today is a very subtle regional one. I am proud that the Negro protest is primarily a Southern protest. I want to claim it as a Southern movement. Heretofore, many Negro Northerners looked down upon their black cousins in the South as not having enough get-up-and-go to come North. They regarded them as country bumpkins.

Those days are over. The very symbol of the protest, Martin Luther King, has a deep rich Southern accent. He can shift that if he needs to, but he has it. He is an Atlanta product. The fact that Negro Southerners have been willing to face police brutality, and hoses, and dogs in order to assert their rights has had an interesting depriving effect on the non-Southern Negro. A man in Harlem says to himself, "That same country cousin, the man I thought was an Uncle Tom, is out there facing Bull Connor; the least I can do is lie down in front of a truck at a building site in Brooklyn." This has had direct consequences for militant action in the North, which followed—it did not initiate—in the temporal sequence of the Negro protest.

The African and regional factors are small effects but they also contribute to relative deprivation. And this is the stuff of which revolutions are made. Revolutions, however, do not occur during periods of hopelessness. They occur during periods of rising aspirations. In fact, rising aspirations are one of the best predictors of revolution. In Panama, it is just now, when aspirations are rising, that there are riots, although the Panama Canal has been there a long time and discrimination against Panamanians by Canal Zone residents has been going on for years. However, we cannot compare the American Negro revolution with other revolutions of the world. This one is different in many ways. It is a reform revolution that can be understood only in connection with the Negro's unique role in American society. It is like revolutions in some respects. It is a shift from legalism to direct action, from narrow objectives to a full-scale attack across the board, from a demand for an abstract equality to demand for a fair share. It is a revolution in the sense that is has changed from pockets of protest to a genuine mass movement across the nation, and across divisions within the Negro community. It has the heightened militancy and urgency of a revolution, and some of its irrationality. America almost doesn't deserve the kind of Negro leadership it now has, after going to such great lengths to prevent the development of these people. But they developed anyway, fortunately for us.

It is a revolution, then, with a difference. It aims to modify, not to overturn the society it confronts. It seeks to amend and not to ravage. To put it in three words—Negroes want in. They do not wish to destroy or deprecate that which they wish to join.

Not only the Negroes in this revolution are occasionally irrational. White liberals, self-designated and otherwise, who consider themselves to be a part of the revolution, frequently can be far more irrational than the Negroes have been today. I recall one particular man, an official of the National Council of the Churches of Christ, who, in the middle of a hose spraying of Negroes in Birmingham, felt the necessity to call a press conference and say that every white Christian in America should go in front of the hoses and be sprayed along with the Negro protestors. At that time, an old Methodist minister, a friend of mine, said that it seemed to him that what the whites ought to do was to turn the water off.

This is a peculiarly conservative revolution with a peculiarly conservative cast, but then Negroes are extremely conservative people; about the only stand they have taken as a group is on race relations, and on that they have been amazingly conservative until recently. It is just this conservative cast of the revolution that gives it a special force. I do not really accept the Myrdal thesis of a conscience conflict that has worked its way right through American history. The most bigoted white Southerner is guilty, it seems to me, at some deeper level. The revolution in its sharpest outline dramatizes this dilemma. First, it makes whites guilty. And since they do not like being made guilty, they do not rush to join the revolution themselves. They may say very sour things about Negroes, but I interpret that partly as symptomatic of the fact that they are having to wrestle with their conscience even a little more. And the revolution is actually bringing this struggle out.

Second, the revolution by and large has the support of the Federal government. The government has let the revolution down badly at times—in Albany, Georgia, and particularly in the Black Belt—but in general, the revolution does have government support, and this makes a strange ally for true revolutionaries.

Third, it is supported in part by dominant American white opinion. Three-fourths of white Americans in the North and West now approve of the Supreme Court desegregation ruling. A majority of white Northerners believe truly in school desegregation, but only if Negroes are not in the majority.

Fourth, even in the South there is a strong feeling of inevitability, which is as effective as approval in getting social change. If you think an event is going to come anyway, you do not resist it as you would otherwise. This inevitability felt by white Southerners does not mean a significant change in the attitude of the South toward desegregation—at least not yet.

Year after year, Gallup has asked, "Do you feel that the day will ever come when Negroes and whites will eat together in public facilities, will go to school together?" He started asking this question quite early in the fifties. By 1957 only 45 per cent of the whites said, yes, the day would come. Today, 83 per cent say the day will come. Apparently, the handwriting on the wall is now so clear that even Southern segregationist illiterates can read it.

Having said that there is basic white support for the revolution at one level, I have immediately to qualify this by saying that there are very serious limitations to this support. On the one hand, there is almost no identification with the Negro on the part of white Americans, certainly not as a mass phenomenon. White

Americans do not even try to think black, even for a few minutes. The dominant white opinion does not sense yet the urgency of the revolution.

This lack of identification and the lack of a sense of urgency limit white support. Over and over one hears the statement that Negroes are pushing too hard, too fast. Such a remark exposes the failure of most white Americans to identify with the Negro's problems. The white American still believes that Negroes are treated fairly in this country and that gradualism should be the rule in racial change.

Naturally, then, a conscience-pricking direct action is resented; it hurts to be reminded, as direct action uniquely does, of the fact that Negroes are not treated fairly. In 1961, 64 per cent of white Americans were against freedom rides, and 57 per cent said it would hurt the Negro's cause. In 1963, 65 per cent of the white North and 73 per cent of the white South said that mass demonstrations would hurt the Negro cause. The late President Kennedy gave the best answer to that argument when in a press conference he was asked whether he thought demonstrations would hurt the Negro cause. He said it had always interested him to note that the people who raise this issue tend to be those who have been against the Negro cause all along and have nothing to lose.

There are four parameters to the present situation: one, severe relative deprivation at the psychological level of the individual Negro. Two, an urgent but a basically conservative revolution. Three, general support by the Federal government for the revolution. And fourth, the guilty, if gradualistic, form of dominant white opinion. In that context, I would like to make six predictions.

First, that Negro protests will continue to grow in intensity and depth. Every advance will make for more relative deprivation. With more success the Negroes will undoubtedly raise their aspiration level further. Reduced frustration will come only when improvements begin to come faster than the aspiration level is increased, and we are nowhere near that point yet.

Consequently even with rapid progress in 1964, we can expect to see greater Negro frustration. This is one way that advances reinforce protests. As one Negro lady said, "We certainly would have liked to bargain it out at the negotiation table. But we tried that for years, and it didn't work and sit-ins did." This is a beautiful psychological statement of reinforcement. You use what works—this has always been a nice American value.

Second, advances will highlight further needed changes. With every improvement other improvements still necessary will become more conspicuous.

Third, we will have what we call in psychology a gradient phenomenon—that is, second wind, the point near the end of an experiment when the subjects, despite their fatigue, tend to pick up and do better. It is a little spurt right at the end. As the revolutionaries begin to see their goals attained, they will experience this phenomenon; they will increase the pressure of their protest because they will be running for home.

The psychological effects of the demonstrations should never be forgotten. You do not leave a public demonstration the same as when you went to it. Participating gives the protester a new sense of political efficacy. The discovery that he can do something about this world, that he is not a hopeless pawn in a chess game is for the Negro both a symptom and a cause of psychological health. A Negro lady in the middle of the Montgomery boycott showed brilliant psychological insight when she said, "My feet are tired but my soul is rested."

In addition, the demonstration teaches disengagement to the protesters. This is a simple idea which we call role reciprocation. It means that there cannot be segregation or discrimination unless both sides play the game, that discrimination involves both the white discriminator and the consenting Negro. If the Negro does not consent, the system breaks down at some level. In a demonstration, the Negro protester learns this. He learns, as labor unions learned long ago, that if he disengages, the system does not work any more.

In this sense, the Negro is practically as guilty as the white for having permitted the situation to continue for this long. But of course the Negro was not in a position to actually disengage. To learn about disengagement, however, to learn that segregation is a two-way street, is a very valuable lesson and supports my hypothesis that the protest will continue to grow in intensity and depth.

Finally, a demonstration teaches the Negro to abandon his Negro role. To be a Negro in the United States is not a matter of a biological category. Incidentally, 25 per cent of all the genes of people who are called Negroes in the United States are Caucasian. To be a Negro really means to play "a Negro role," to know one's place, to be, or pretend to be, servile, stupid, and happy-go-lucky.

A public demonstration for desegregation takes the Negro role and stands it on its head. A protester does everything the other way. And the Negro learns how to be a first class citizen at the same time that he is winning his first class citizenship. If young people from Harlem go to Mississippi to work for the Negro vote, to risk their lives for the vote, they will never miss an election. This experience is similar to that of Alcoholics Anonymous, which sends an ex-alcoholic to help a new alcoholic who wants help. We don't think the help to the new alcoholic is of much value except for bringing him to the group. What is really valuable is what happens to the ex-alcoholic who increases his determination not to drink. He convinces himself; he plays a new role and gets reinforcement for his conviction.

My fourth prediction is that the protest will increasingly attract a larger proportion of Negroes from lower income homes and will shift from status to economic goals. A truly mass movement must finally involve lower class Negroes, and as it does, economic goals will become more critical.

Fifth, I predict a more extensive use of local and national boycotts of consumer products. Twenty per cent of the people in the *Newsweek* poll said they had already boycotted some product or store; sixty-three per cent said they were willing to boycott; and over two-thirds of the richest Negroes in the sample said they were willing to boycott.

A boycott has two special advantages in the Negro revolution. One is economic: it is an immediate leverage on their most important problem, employment. The second advantage is psychological. A boycott appeals to each one of the dominant psychological reactions to oppression. To put it crudely, there are three things you can do when you are oppressed: you can withdraw and try to avoid the oppressor, a course many Negroes follow rather stringently; you can move against attack and be aggressive, as the Muslims do to a certain point; or you can move away and seek acceptance in some way, which is the dominant Negro American response reflected in such organizations as the NAACP and the Urban League.

The boycott has the unique advantage of appealing to all three of these dominant reactions. It appeals to Negroes of many different personality types. Move toward—certainly, because the aim of the protest is integration. Move against—certainly, because it upsets the white man's economy and thereby appeals to hostile antiwhite feelings. Move away—yes, for you do not ask the boycotter to go down and picket but only to stay away from the scene of conflict.

Sixth and last, I predict that as the reform movement proceeds through the 1960s, some basic structural changes in American society will have to occur before viable race relation solutions are possible. These changes include wider employment, a different taxation base, an extension of the minimum wage to cover service workers, and massive retraining. Clearly, the problem we are trying to solve transcends the boundaries of civil rights and reaches into the basic structure of American society.

I would like to end with a question. Can the revolution deal as effectively with de facto segregation in educational and employment as it has dealt with legal segregation?

This is an earlier version of chapter Eight of A PROFILE OF THE NEGRO AMERICAN *by Thomas F. Pettigrew, published by D. Van Nostrand Company, Inc., Princeton, New Jersey, 1964, and is reprinted by permission of the publisher.*

THE NEGRO IN TURMOIL

Kenneth C. Clark

Inevitably, the Negro protest movement, like every other human movement, contains the stabilizing factor of humor. On the other hand, it faces the insidious threat of being drowned in words. We, particularly those of us in academic life, may be preparing to talk this movement into immobility and stagnation. And I suppose I might as well make my contribution to this immobilization.

What can we say about social protest? It is an endless quest for justice, decency, all the things we have fought for since the beginning of recorded history and even before. The search becomes so extended that after a while we reach the point where almost anything we say must be trite. We feel like the student who says, "Don't human beings know this? Don't people know that if other people are treated unjustly there will be resentment, anger, confusion? Did the Americans in the Panama Canal Zone not know that decade after decade of flagrant discrimination and injustice would lead to flare-up?"

This reminds me of a horrifying experience I had with my son, who is now a sophomore at Columbia University. After I tell you of this experience, you will know that his role at that particular university is not an easy one. When he was about fourteen years old I took him with me on a speaking engagement. I spoke before an assembly meeting of the Ethical Society in Philadelphia on the psychological consequences of racial prejudice and discrimination. At the end of the meeting, we had a coffee hour and the audience was very gracious. Each person came up and told me how much he enjoyed my talk. I tried to smile, and I wondered how anyone could enjoy what I had said if he had listened.

But I decided to play the etiquette game of the invited speaker who speaks graciously to those who compliment him. After some minutes of this, I looked around for my son but could not find him. When I finally found him downstairs I suggested that we leave. He said that he had been ready for a long time.

When I asked him how he had enjoyed the talk, my fourteen-year-old son looked at me with a terrifying, unctuous smile. He came up, took my hand, and said, "Dr. Clark, I want to tell you how much I enjoyed your talk. I learned a very complex thing this morning. I learned that Negroes are human beings, too, and that if you are cruel to them they react the way other human beings react."

I was sick—sick at the penetrating, devastating truth my son had imposed upon me, and which has not left me since. Needless to say, he is having trouble. He is having trouble in this society because he would not accept my contention that if one is to survive one has to deal with the problems and frailties of human beings without the kind of crushing severity my son brought to the situation.

To return to the protest movement. This one, like all others, comes out of a long-standing pattern of injustice, cruelty, inconsistency, and indifference. We all know the history of racial and national persecution that has run its paradoxical course beside the other story of America's effort to hammer out a system of government based upon democratic ideology.

In its contemporary form this protest movement is an intensification of the conflict caused by white resistance to Negro demands. It is a counterresistance—a dramatic one—which the Negro is now using to obtain his goals. This manifest level of the Negro protest movement has understandably obscured some of the more profound human problems involved in a rapid transition from a racially segregated to a nonsegregated society.

I would like to spend a few moments considering not the manifest and obvious, the more easily recognizable level of the protest movement, but the repressed aspects of the problem. When the cries of anguish and the threats of violence from the segregationists subside, as I believe they will, I hope that the protest movement will be resolved positively in the direction of the American creed, although I think that some of the evidence we selectively push aside does not insure this outcome. Let us look at the Negro in this movement and see what will confront him by way of inner anxieties, conflicts, and challenges as he moves beyond the manifest level of this protest. If he does not move beyond the manifest level of the protest—past the demonstration stage—then the protest movement will have failed. For the continuation of the inevitable techniques of transition means failure.

Let us assume that these techniques do work. Then the signs of their working will bring additional problems for the Negro as he seeks to strengthen and stabilize his society. It will then be more clear that the problems of adjusting to this change are not only difficult for whites but in various insidious ways quite difficult and disturbing for Negroes. A segregated society not only damages people but, in a curiously debilitating way, also protects them.

The more responsible organizational leadership among Negroes cannot easily face this fact or even admit it. It may, therefore, be one of the roles of a Negro who has no such responsibility, who does not have to play up to the group and meet the demands of the protest movement, to think of this. But the worlds of the segregated society are quite constrictive and damaging, specifically as they protect mediocrity, inferiority, apathy, and explanations of personal inadequacies in terms of very real patterns of racial injustice. It would be politically and socially impossible if not suicidal for responsible Negro leaders to admit that the injustice of racism must be seen and understood in terms of its corroding effect on human beings.

In the transition, however, a group must move beyond the tactics of revolution. How can one understand the essence of the human problems and difficulties the American Negro will be required to face and solve as he moves closer to his goal of equality in a non-segregated society without understanding the detrimental effects of racial segregation on the personality of Negroes and of whites.

A system of racism and segregation corrodes the human spirit from the first conscious awareness that one is rejected and stigmatized because of the color of one's skin. This is an intimate aspect of self which the individual is powerless to change. In order to understand the present and future dilemmas of the American Negro, we must first understand one of the nuclear, essential things about racism: it makes the individual so doubt himself in his own world that he must thereafter struggle to develop some reasonable positive sense of self in order to function with any degree of effectiveness.

It is a reasonable hypothesis, supported by overwhelming empirical evidence, that no Negro and probably no white in America is able to escape some effect of racism as he seeks to function as a human being. Such effects probably permeate every aspect of his personal relationships—including his marital and sexual relationships and his vocational and professional life. This suggests the shocking possibility that a problem of social injustice can in fact be so all pervasive as to permeate if not to dominate all aspects of an individual's life.

One of the major challenges therefore confronting the American Negro is the need to find some adequate protection and defense against this intolerable state of pervasive psychological and racial oppression. Among the possible defenses open to him are those of denial, repression, and withdrawal. Another is the defense taken by the upwardly mobile Negroes who insist that racial problems are either nonexistent or easily thrown off, or that they are the consequence of the behavior of uncouth, unclean, undramatic Negroes. Still another defense may be the frantic desire of the individual Negro to lose himself in his music, his church, or his recreation, wherein he is cushioned at least temporarily from the assaulting, abrasive white world.

Specifically, if you gentlemen were to announce tomorrow that you have a completely open employment policy, your doors would not be flooded by hundreds of Negroes with high self-esteem and high aspiration, coming in to demonstrate to you that they are competent, faithful, and equal to meet the competition of your other workers. This is a level of unrealism which we in academia, and certainly the responsible professional leaders, too often encourage.

Another challenge that will confront the American Negro will be the impatience he will feel with existing forms of discrimination as he moves closer to the goal of a nonsegregated society. For racial justice and equality must be understood primarily in terms of an all-or-none principle, with all of its complications, confusions, and inconsistencies. The American creed has been voiced often enough to have finally taken root. The contention that a group either enjoys justice and equality or it does not is a major American contribution to the issue of human and social justice, and this literalistic approach to democracy, with all its ambivalences and conflicts, has oddly enough been accepted by the Negro.

The principle is extremely difficult for white moderates and, interestingly enough, some white liberals, to grasp. The persistent advice that Negroes should pace their demands for unqualified rights as American citizens reflects this difficulty in understanding that when a human being is different and obtains, through his own efforts or the efforts of others close to him or through sacrifices, some of his rights, his appetite is then whetted for all the rights and responsibilities that other groups in the same social system enjoy.

As the lines of racial confrontation become more clearly drawn, some of the basic dilemmas of the Negro people take the form of apparent ideological differences and conflicts. Here again, the present state of the Negro protest movement is reflected in the ideological differences and conflicts among the various protest groups. The most obvious one of these differences is found in the relationship between the tactics and the philosophy of Martin Luther King, on the one hand, and the Black Muslim movement on the other. On the surface, these two approaches appear to be dramatically and diametrically opposed. Martin Luther King preaches a doctrine of love for the oppressed, while at the same time offering a very effective social action technique of nonviolent, assertive demand for Negro rights equal to those of any other American citizen.

The Black Muslims preach a doctrine of black supremacy, hatred of whites, and total separation of Negroes from whites. The whites, in the Black Muslim verbalisms, are characterized as morally defective and therefore incapable of offering Negroes justice and equality.

This is the manifest level of comparison and, on the manifest level, there is an obvious difference. In spite of these apparent differences, however, it would be a mistake to ignore the similarities between these two movements. Each reflects the Negro's basic impatience. Each accepts the assumption that if the Negro is to attain his rights, he must do so primarily if not exclusively through his own efforts. And I think this is true in spite of a verbal, tactical tendency to obscure this on the part of both King and the Muslims. Basically, both groups have in common a kind of Negro nationalism; the Muslim, of course, is more flagrantly nationalistic than King and his colleagues, whose appeals are more subtle and sophisticated.

The most significant similarity between these two movements, however, is the fact that they represent a basic dilemma, an ambivalence within the Negro people as a whole. The Black Muslims reflect the reality of hatred and resentment that Negroes understandably feel toward white oppressors. The Muslims are honest and verbally defiant in their extreme expression of this genuine and understandable human reaction to injustice. The fact that they might be unrealistic, inconsistent, and even verbally inhumane in the remedy they suggest, and quite threatening and frightening in their stark unalloyed racism, is not particularly relevant to the understanding of the psychological reality that the Muslims reflect, namely, the reality of racism as an aspect of the American culture. They present the mirrored image of the garden-variety, respectable racism that liberal, tolerant, re-spectable whites have managed to accept as long as the victim, or the intended victim, was black. When it is suggested, however, that the victim might be white, anxiety mounts and the mass media explode with indignation over the Black Muslims.

Martin Luther King also reflects an aspect of this general feeling of Negroes for whites. It is not possible for two groups to have shared a common destiny for over 300 years without certain bonds of identity and affect developing. This, in spite of pervading problems of injustice. Particularly is this true with the Negro-white relationship in America, a relationship that was well described by a rather casual statement James Baldwin once made when I asked him during the course of a television interview about the principal in his school in Harlem. It was a typical American question: Was the principal white or Negro? Baldwin looked at me with that wonderful sophisticated naïvete of his and said, "She was like you, a little bit white and a little bit Negro."

Of course every American Negro is a little bit white and little bit black, and an undetermined number of American whites are also a little bit white and a little bit black, and therein might lie a deeply disturbing, psychoanalytic, psychological rub. Certainly the problems of the mixture and the sexual and racial

complexities are disturbing. The Puritan verbalism that domi-
nates so much of American society makes quite complicated the
presence of a group that is both rejected and related. As an
experimental social psychologist I am not always sure that man
will be able to develop a rational technique for dealing with the
terribly disturbing, threatening, and confusing irrationalities in
the system.

An inescapable reality, however, is that the American Negro is
inextricably American. This probably accounts for the fact that
this is a peculiar type of revolution, for it is not seeking to destroy
or to overturn, but merely to share. The American Negro is
merely asking to share in whatever exists in America today, including its emptiness.

In my work with the youngsters in Harlem, I can always get
a rise out of them, particularly when they get too aggressive
toward me, by asking them whether, in a sense, they aren't asking
that we change the statistics of deprivation, including the suicide
statistics? When they ask what I mean, I remind them that the
one factor the Negro population has on its side in terms of all
the indications of pathology is its suicide rate, which is lower
that that of the whites. I tell the youngsters, "You must understand that once we level all the other indications of pathology,
the suicide rate among Negroes is going to increase." If one
wanted to be as disturbing as my son was in Philadelphia, one
could say that the American Negro in the protest movement is
asking that his suicide rate increase to a rate that is equal to that
of the American white, or that he be able to become alcoholic
with the same brand of alcoholism as the whites.

Let us consider where we go from here. The burden of the
Negro on the manifest level of his protest is to develop an
effective technique for bringing into the consciousness of the
American white the need to develop that degree of maturity
which is essential for a truly democratic society. The optimist
among the observers of this protest would have felt that August 28, 1963, was a demonstration of the potential success and

effectiveness of the Negro's campaign, because on August 28 the march on Washington demonstrated the seriousness, the discipline, and the persistence with which American Negroes and many whites were insisting that racial injustices and cruelties must now be eliminated from American life.

Even at the time, however, there was again a curious kind of detachment, a stepping back to look at the demonstration in terms of the actuality of political power. The fact that it had occurred, and occurred without violence, seemed to indicate that by some magic the goals would be attained. But after the year of confrontation, it was perhaps to be expected that America, with its admirable flexibility, would return to business as usual. The following illustrations of this business-as-usual approach to the problem underscore the trouble we face in terms of basic change.

An orderly political process that allows filibusters to proceed without any major outcry from the business, religious, or educational communities of America seems to be a subtle, or not so subtle, sign of return to business as usual, in spite of the march and in spite of the nature of the confrontation during 1963.

A situation in which labor unions could eliminate their racial exclusion clauses and remain free to exclude Negroes effectively from the more skilled and better paid work force suggests no major change of attitude. The elimination of the exclusion clauses is particularly effective since in the forefront of those unions that continue the practice of exclusion are liberal, efficient, noncorrupt unions, good unions that contribute significantly to the Liberal Party. But the fact of Negro exclusion remains despite the guise of liberalism and verbal changes. This can happen and probably will happen unless we develop something other than the manifest level of protest.

Another index of business as usual, and therefore another signal of the futility of the protest movement, might be found among those employers who sign nondiscrimination contracts, pledge to cooperate with presidential committees, and then show their good faith by hiring highly selected Negroes to function as adjuncts to personnel departments or to give advice on how one should not change basic hiring policies because that would be preferential treatment and unfair. The Negro thus remains in his servile job and responsible Negro leaders are immobilized by token verbal changes rather than any fundamental changes in the patterns of employment.

Again, where banks and real estate institutions can perpetuate racial residential sanctuaries and ghettos, and, in fact, go as far as they can without announcing publicly that they are violating the law, we cannot say that basic change is under way. Clearly, Americans must be very careful about the ease with which they make verbal, surface changes without getting at the substantive, more difficult and painful level of social change. This is not a peculiarly white affliction. Negroes are also Americans, and Negro leaders were really willing to settle, whether they now remember and admit it or not, for this kind of tokenism before the students who hadn't learned how to be sophisticated in the American way exploded with their sit-ins.

Tokenism will allow school boards to maintain their racially segregated schools provided there are a few highly selected, nice Negro children who are permitted to attend designated white schools, and provided that racially segregated schools are all neighborhood schools or special schools for dull, or for brilliant, or for particularly difficult children. Negroes will continue to live in substandard or deteriorated housing as long as their conditions are made more desperate by urban renewal and displacement projects. Negroes will continue to be rebuffed and humiliated and to be made uncertain about their reception in places of public accommodation as long as they disturb the peace, or in some way violate the sacred constitutionally guaranteed rights of private property.

If any of this were allowed to happen, it would be the result of serious miscalculations and misinterpretations of the meaning of the protest movement. I do not believe we will settle for that level of verbal manipulation again. Because of the very stark predicament of their lives, Negroes cannot permit themselves now to settle for verbal rather than actual changes.

Ways must be found therefore to make the Congress of the United States and the state legislatures more sensitive and responsive to the present mood of urgent realism which is deeper within the Negro masses than at any other time in our history. Serious negotiations with the leaders of American labor movements and the leaders of individual unions must be initiated and sustained. And if these discussions do not result in the elimination of patterns of racial exclusion from the American labor movement, then more direct action techniques appropriate and specific to this particular area of discrimination, which is looming larger and larger, must be developed by responsible Negro organizations or groups. This must be done because so much of the economic ills of the Negro reflect primarily, and ironically, the resistance of labor to racial democracy.

More systematic, organized, and sustained forms of selective patronage on the part of Negroes must be developed and used in order to eliminate racial discrimination in employment and public accommodations. Effective forms of selective patronage have been developed in enough different parts of the nation so that all that is required now is systematic planning and intelligent organization rather than *ad hoc* approaches. We hope that the Negro organizations will come to recognize the need for systematic, intelligent organization so that events will not determine techniques.

The problem of residential segregation must be attacked by the development of an appropriate and effective form of direct protest against the discriminatory practices of banks and real estate groups. Again, I am suggesting that we need to develop a specific technique for a particular problem area rather than rely on blanket protests and banner waving, which cannot deal with these difficult and stubborn areas.

Police brutality must be curbed, and law enforcement agencies must be taught that it is their duty to protect all citizens impartially. If this cannot be done by reason, then it must be done by appropriate forms of intelligently planned, disciplined, and highly specific forms of simple disobedience.

Apathy, indifference, battle weariness and wishful thinking are some of the major dangers which must be counteracted in the next stage of the civil rights struggle. The momentum of the Negroes' search for equality as American citizens during the past few years, and particularly during the past year, has not only been admirable and miraculous, it has also been exhausting. The demonstrations of the past cannot be permitted to be meaningless. The determination of the protestors must be sustained by intelligent, hard talk and by the development of techniques and methods appropriate to the area.

This requires at least the following: First, the organization of an effective machinery consisting of representatives of the major civil rights groups. No such machinery now exists, although the groups are loosely linked by good working relationships among individuals. There is, of course, some value to flexibility, but there must be some optimum balance between flexibility and coordination. Such a coordinating body must be vested with power to apply over-all strategy, define specific targets, determine techniques of protests, supply roles and responsibilities, initiate negotiations, make decisions, and maintain discipline among the participants of the protest movement.

Very closely related to this is the need to develop a more precise and forthright agreement over the role of white allies of Negroes in this civil rights movement. The white involvement in the civil rights movement has been a most heartening and positive development; it has also been an interesting and complicated one. White groups are apparently quite welcome in all civil rights groups except the Muslims as long as they share the risks and the goals of unqualified rights for American Negro citizens.

Problems may develop, however, if there are any attempts at

present for white groups to confuse these goals or to attempt to qualify them as a price for continued friendship. Possibly there will be a period of major infighting between Negro groups and white liberal groups in the near future. This is an aspect of the larger war, the battle that only independent Negro intellectuals can take on with the white erstwhile friends of the Negro.

Finally, we must develop a program designed to educate the masses of Negroes to use effectively and intelligently the new opportunities we hope will be open to them. Such a program should include at least youth training and educational reorientation and development, vocational training and retraining for adolescents and adults, information about health, nutrition, and family life, and adult education. Above all, we need a program on voter registration and political community responsibility.

POLITICAL PERSPECTIVES

Daniel Patrick Moynihan

Much of the public, which rarely pays close attention to politics from one election to the next, has a narrow view of the politician's freedom of choice. If they like what he does, he's a statesman; if they don't, he's a "politician"—with the quotation marks usually indicated by a curl of the lip.

They rarely consider the matter of political necessity, which is not necessarily a matter of political selfishness or self-interest. There are national necessities to which any politician worthy of the name must bow in the name of the national interest. We all recognize this aspect of political behavior when it comes to nonpartisan support of the party in power during wartime or bipartisanship in critical areas of foreign policy. The public is less likely to recognize this phenomenon of political behavior where domestic affairs are concerned, admittedly because that is an area where partisanship is more untrammeled.

I will try to describe from the viewpoint of a working member of one of the political parties certain trends of the past fifteen to twenty years that are now accepted as political facts by both parties, facts that exert, in other words, virtually the same pressure on and will elicit the same response from the political executives and the legislators of both major parties.

We tend to think there is a great difference between our parties. Indeed, we like to think we have a great range of choice among candidates. Certainly there are differences. But it is my experience, and I think I can say it is the consensus among people in politics, that there are some circumstances in which all responsible political executives must respond in about the same way. This is particularly the case in the critical domestic issue of what place the Negro is now to take in American society.

The point made to you here by Eli Ginzberg is fundamental. Until quite recently, America has been virtually a whites-only democracy. A democracy, but a white democracy. The Negroes have been here longer than most other ethnic groups, but they have not been a significant part of the democratic system. The reaction of the political parties to their present agitation therefore comes as a surprise to many people. Those most surprised are those least involved in politics.

Clearly, many people wonder about the political motivations behind what is going on in civil rights. Why, they ask, is civil rights suddenly such an overriding issue? The answer couldn't be simpler. It is the basic answer to any such question in American government: civil rights is suddenly a major political issue in America because the Negroes have begun to vote. ("Suddenly," of course, here means the last fifteen years, not the past several months.)

In 1940, when most of the Negroes lived in the South, there were only about 250,000 registered Negro voters in the South. This was about 5 per cent of the South's voting-age Negro population. In the South today, 28 per cent of the Negroes are registered voters. Without question, the Negro voter will become an important factor by 1970.

More important for understanding the present is the fact that Negroes have moved into the North—into the Northern cities, the centers of the political, intellectual, and economic life of the country. They have begun to vote there because voting is encouraged and easy. It is part of the political tradition of these cities to get out the vote, not to restrict it; in fact, the competition to get out the vote for one party or the other is characteristic and fierce. Historically, the Democratic party has responded more actively to immigrant groups than the Republicans have, but it is a political practice common to both parties.

The number of Negro voters outside the South rose from about 2 million in 1950 to more than 3 million in 1960, and it is going up steadily. Meanwhile, the Negro population in the South has dropped from 30 per cent of the total Southern population in 1950 to 20 per cent in 1960. Thus we now have a situation in which eight of the key industrial states of the nation, states whose votes normally determined who is going to be President, have a large segment of Negro voters. They are 10 per cent of the population in Illinois; 9 per cent in Michigan and Missouri; 8 per cent in New York, New Jersey, Pennsylvania, and Ohio; 6 per cent in California. And they are voting. The state with the largest number of Negroes is New York. In 1960 approximately 1,400,000 Negroes lived in New York: the figure is probably 1,600,000 today. Even in the South, where the Negro vote has not heretofore been a political factor of any considerable importance, the emergence of the two-party system is suddenly making the Negro vote a key issue in national politics.

John F. Kennedy could look to ten states in this country, including several in the South, and say that if he hadn't won the Negro vote in those states he wouldn't have been President. Richard Nixon could look to those same ten states and say that if he had come anywhere near splitting the Negro vote, he would have been President.

Kennedy won Texas by 45,000 votes. There were 100,000 Negro votes in that state, of which 95 per cent were probably cast for him. North Carolina went for Kennedy by a margin of

58,000 votes. In that state, he got an estimated 70,000 Negro votes. He won South Carolina by less than 10,000 votes. In that state, 40,000 Negro votes were cast, again probably overwhelmingly for him. If Kennedy had received 8,000—even 6,000—fewer Negro votes in South Carolina, he might not have been President.

Even in the South, the Negro vote can switch from one party to another and one issue to another. When a group can direct its influence in this manner, it obtains power in a democracy. That is how power is meant to be exercised in America—through the ballot.

Probably most important from the point of view of a political party is the fact that the Negro has become overwhelmingly urban, as well as increasingly Northern. In 1960, for the first time in history, the Negroes of America were more urban than the whites: 73.2 per cent of the Negroes in the country were living in cities, while 69.5 per cent of the white population were urban.

Moreover, Negroes are increasingly concentrated in the major cities, the cities that really affect American life. In the decade of the 1980s, seven of the ten largest cities in America will almost certainly come to have Negro majorities. Washington, the nation's capital, already has a Negro majority. Detroit, Cleveland, Baltimore, Chicago, St. Louis, and Philadelphia are heading that way. On the other hand, New York, Los Angeles, and Houston are likely to retain white majorities, at least in this century.

This increase will occur in more than urban areas. Negroes are becoming a larger proportion of the total population than they used to be. At the time of the Civil War, Negroes were 14 per cent of the population; by 1930 they had dropped to 9.7 per cent. A higher death rate among Negroes than among whites and extensive white immigration contributed to lowering the Negro proportion of the population. It has been rising since 1930, however, so that by 1960 Negroes made up 10.6 per cent of the nation. The birth rate among Negroes in America today is almost half again as great as that of whites. And their death rate has dropped almost to that of whites.

As a consequence, we are seeing constant changes in voting patterns and election results. In every new election things happen for the first time. In 1962, for example, the people of the Commonwealth of Massachusetts elected a Negro attorney general. He is a Republican. The treasurer of Connecticut, who I believe is a Democrat, is a Negro. The people of Michigan recently elected a Negro justice to their State Supreme Court. The people of Alabama recently elected a Negro state senator. There are five Negro congressmen sitting in the House of Representatives today. They are all Democrats, but that is probably a consequence of their all being urbanites rather than the expression of any inflexible rule.

Given these results of the Negro's growing political role in American life, one would expect the racial conflict to be abating. With increasing political power should come growing economic strength, which ought in turn to result in a relaxation of racial tension as Negro civil rights activists taper off their public demonstrations in the wake of their success. That this is not the case is largely explained by the Negro's economic frustration as he seeks to raise his income and reduce the rate of his unemployment.

At every level of government on which I have worked during the past dozen years, and my experience includes city, state, and Federal posts, I have sensed the Negroes' consciousness of their growing power as voters. But this sense of power contrasts increasingly with a feeling of frustration as to what that power is achieving for them. They feel their conditions are not getting sufficiently better.

Even though Negroes can swing the nomination and election of a Negro attorney general in Massachusetts and a Negro borough president in Manhattan, they are having increasing difficulty simply finding employment. As he moves upward, the Negro is encountering far more structural resistance than he anticipated.

In the last decade or so, the Negro's economic position has been falling relatively farther behind that of the white's. He has not been closing the gap. The gap has, in fact, been widening in terms of comparative employment and earnings. In 1951, after raising his average income for a number of years, the Negro male wage earner was making 62 per cent of the wage his white equivalent was making. By 1962, he had dropped back to 55 per cent.

Negroes went through a good period of catching up during World War II. Between 1939 and 1947 they picked up 13 percentage points. They moved from earning 41 per cent as much as whites to 54 per cent. By 1951, they were up to 62 per cent, but now they have dropped back to about 55 per cent. The spread, in other words, is growing wider again. The fifteen years from 1947 to 1962 therefore showed a net improvement of only 1 per cent. If the trend continues, in two or three years Negroes may be relatively further behind whites than they were in 1947.

It is important to keep in mind that the Negro's relative decline of seven percentage points occurred between 1951 and 1962, which were good years in this country. During this time, the average annual income of male Negro workers increased by $963 while the average income of the white worker went up $2,117. That is not closing the gap; it is widening the gap.

The situation in terms of employment has been much the same. We have reached a point at which, in terms of unemployment, the working rule is that, compared to whites, Negroes have double the trouble. Unemployment figures for December, 1963, show a national unemployment rate for whites of 4.7 per cent during December; for Negroes, it was 10 per cent. For the whole year 1963, the average unemployment rate was 5.1 per cent for whites and 10.9 per cent for Negroes.

Twice as much unemployment would not be so difficult to accept if previously it had been treble. This would at least be some progress. But it wasn't treble before. In 1948-1953, the Negroes had 1.7 times the rate of unemployment of the whites.

In 1954-1962 it was up to 2.1 times. It is getting worse. And the worst area, where it is an especially acute problem for both Negroes and whites, is among youth.

Youth unemployment is not simply a Negro problem but a problem affecting all youngsters because of the direction the economy is taking. Negro youngsters, however, are affected the most. From 1953 to 1964 youth unemployment rose from 6.3 per cent to 11 per cent for white male teen-agers, and from 7.1 per cent to 11.7 per cent for Negro male teen-agers. Among girls, the period from 1953 to 1964 saw the unemployment rate for white teen-agers go from 5.4 per cent to 9.3 per cent and for Negro teen-agers from 7.5 per cent to 17.1 per cent.

Moreover, youth unemployment was not just a few percentage points higher than the adult rate; it had started getting much higher. During this past year the employment level in America has not worsened radically. It was about 5½ per cent throughout the year. But twice during the year we reached a new unemployment peak for teen-agers, the highest rates we have ever recorded. In 1963, the unemployment rate for teenage male and female whites was 14 per cent; for Negro male and female teen-agers it was 28.4 per cent. This is large-scale unemployment. It is unemployment beyond the imagination of most people.

The impression of our technicians in the Department of Labor is that in three or four years the unemployment rates for Negro teen-agers could also be experienced by white teen-agers if present trends and conditions continue. But the Negroes are not finding much consolation in the thought that things will soon be just as difficult for whites. They know they have a special problem and that it has been getting worse.

To be out of work completely is worse than to be working at a low wage. The Negro community knows that it is casting youngsters into the work force who are practically unemployable, who are so ill-trained, ill-motivated, and ill-situated that their expectations are virtually nil. Even among those who go through school, few graduate with useful skills. It is not their fault but the fault of their schools, and we must recognize the inadequate quality of these schools if we are to understand why the Negroes are putting forward such pressure for better education.

Negroes are not only voting in this country today, but they are also asserting their other constitutional rights. In lawsuit after lawsuit, they have obtained rulings from the highest court in the land on what their rights are. Without any question, the key decision was *Brown v. Board of Education* in 1954, in which the Court stated that separate but equal school systems are not acceptable, that school systems have to be desegregated.

This was a clear confrontation between Negroes and whites: the Supreme Court had ordered desegregation; what were the whites going to do about it? The answer is that not much has been done. Of the Negro students in the states of the old Confederacy, 1.6 per cent are in integrated schools; 99 per cent are still in the same segregated schools they were in when the Supreme Court spoke out a decade ago. Up North, where we do not avowedly discriminate by race, 90 per cent of all Negro youngsters are in comparably segregated elementary schools in Harlem, Brownsville, and similar Negro ghettos, and it does not seem to many Negroes that much can be done about it. The courts have spoken, but the Negroes aren't getting their due. The disappointed reaction of any group in such a situation is easy enough to understand.

Ironically, the Negroes are achieving political power at a time when many of the immediately profitable advantages of political power are being taken away. It used to be that if your party became the political majority in a city, or if you won the mayor's office, or the borough presidency, all the politically controlled jobs were yours. But now that a Negro is finally the borough president of Manhattan, for example, it turns out that a Negro who wants a job as a clerk or inspector or whatever has to take an examination. Civil service has dried up many of the former sources of employment.

At a time when most of the people in this country are making more money than ever, we have many people who are property-less in the most personal sense. They possess no education, no position, no connections. Our economic system isn't using them.

This is a problem American business must face. If American business doesn't face it, we could become the kind of country that you and I don't want, that nobody wants, but that's the way it might turn out. Let me illustrate with several blunt facts about employment. Since 1947, more than one out of every three jobs added to the American work force has been in government at the Federal, state, or local level. Since 1957, 46 per cent of the jobs added to the American work force have been in state and local government. Only in this area has employment been growing substantially.

The Federal government will continue to move forward, will continue to seek by legislation as much as can be achieved by legislation. President Johnson, in his State of the Union message, said, "Let this session of Congress be known as the session which did more for civil rights than the last hundred sessions combined." Political reality requires such an effort, but it is equally necessary for the national welfare.

I have tried to explain what may seem to be the dollars-and-cents politics of civil rights. But I think there is something more important than these practical political considerations. And that is the fact that the American conscience has now been engaged on this subject. Whatever we say about ourselves on occasion, we are a good country, a good people. We are moral people, we are religious people.

The civil rights issue began well over a century ago. It was not begun by the businessman. It was not begun by the Negro. It was begun by the pricking conscience of this nation, which would not stand for slavery. Today, a very similar attitude, this time with the Negro himself very much involved, carries the struggle forward. The civil rights struggle is simultaneously conducted on very practical and very morally elevated levels.

Just as I say that the politics of the situation makes it necessary to accommodate to the Negro's demand for civil rights, I say even more forcefully that the more important fact is that the strength of American moral conviction will make it happen. Above and beyond whatever we take to be the economic demands, the political necessities, the social imperatives, what will finally effect this change is the fact that the American conscience is aroused. Ultimately, it is likely to be the American moral sense that brings us through this time of trial.

REPORTS OF CORPORATE ACTION

The Conference Group

As indicated in the Preface, the primary aim of the Conference was to provide an educational setting for the acquisition of new knowledge and perspective concerning the many complex impacts of the civil rights movement on business. Another aim of the Conference was to provide a congenial environment for members of the Conference to interchange views on the many different ways in which their organizations had responded to the civil rights movement and to assess the strengths and weaknesses inherent in these different types of action and reaction.

These interchanges took place in four discussion groups. At the final session of the Conference a summary report was made by a representative of each group in which he set forth the principal points that had emerged. These are reproduced below with the names of the companies removed.

Our group, by and large, took this conference in the spirit in which it was introduced, as an educational experience. We did not try to solve any problems during our session; instead, we used the opportunity to review some points of view, particularly some questions concerning company practices, and in one or two instances to consider some of the philosophical implications underlying the free enterprise system.

One theme ran throughout our session: the belief that the problem under discussion is not going to be solved by any given date; that, rather, it is going to continue to be with us as a basic part of our economic structure and way of life for a long time to come. One of our group suggested that in reality we might have a kind of national coexistence. But the solution ultimately lies in total integration, whereby corporate officers, executives, the supervisory force, and even employees adopt real integration as a basic way of living—not in anticipation of problems, not in anticipation of crises, but in anticipation of this as a way of living together for the rest of our days, the rest of our country's history.

In our group, because we are business people, we focused on jobs. But it was repeatedly acknowledged that the problem is not confined to employment, that housing, social opportunities, and educational facilities will all have to be improved. Today increasingly, social scientists, representatives of minority groups, educators, and the public are for the first time pointing the finger at business. To some extent this is a recognition of the public service our leading industries and business leaders are now providing. Nevertheless, we must not try to do the total job ourselves. Business should attempt to muster the other forces that have to be mustered to solve housing and educational problems as well.

We reviewed both the specific actions companies are taking and the over-all plans for progress, which include those educational programs within organizations that are aimed at full integration. We went from there to a consideration of the large contributions some companies are making in the form of executive time, funds, money, and support of the integration movement wherever it touches on their operations.

A member of one organization spoke about its lending supervisory and executive staff to counsel and tutor the underprivileged, the children—for the most part, Negro children—of individuals who were on the relief rolls in one of our major cities. This was an example of community-company corporation.

Another representative spoke of working with a Negro group to take functional illiterates off the unemployment rolls in order to train them in the basic skills of reading, writing, and communicating, and then to apply programmed learning techniques to train them in a short period for low-level blue collar jobs.

And another member mentioned a drop-out prevention program now under way in a number of the cities. In this, cooperating companies have agreed to divide among them from twenty to several hundred school drop-outs—again for the most part Negroes—and to give them part-time employment with their organizations to achieve two ends: one, to put them back in school, to encourage them to complete their education and not become a statistic in the juvenile delinquent ranks; and two, to train them for jobs even while they are completing high school.

All the members of our group spoke of 1963 as having been a year that will have a substantial impact on this problem. During this year, for example, one very large organization, which has been employing Negroes on a wide basis for more than twenty years, took on the challenge of establishing an equitable promotion system.

The climate has changed almost totally insofar as white collar employment is concerned. With the possible exception of a specific problem in union relations that has not been solved in one company, the reluctance to employ Negroes, to integrate them in the work force, has been overcome. The log jam has been broken.

Our group talked about a number of the problems that we in industry will have to face and do something about if we are going to meet the challenges that confront us.

The speakers suggested that industry will have to discriminate somewhat against the whites in order to make up for the disadvantages foisted on the Negroes for so many years. But those of us in industry who are responsible for making an adequate return on our investments will find it difficult to depart from the selection standards and procedures we have found most useful in getting the best qualified personnel possible to produce the goods we have to produce.

We can show conclusively that there is a shortage of Negroes adequately trained to fill the positions that may be open from time to time. We have been encouraged to engage in special training programs for people who fall somewhat short of our standards for new employees. Mr. Whitney Young earlier described a program under which forty people who fell slightly short of meeting the selection standards were put through an accelerated training program. Thirty-seven out of the forty met the employment requirements of a number of employers and were then employed by them. This demonstrates, first, that through accelerated training of that kind, people can be made qualified to fill jobs that may be open. But it also proves that, given qualified Negroes, industry will employ them.

The view of our group can be summarized by the statement in Mr. Silberman's *Fortune* article:

A few companies have tried modifying their employment and promotion procedures. When the Negro boycotts were under way in Philadelphia last year, for example, the president of one major corporation decided to take a look at his company's position in advance of any attack. He discovered that his Negro employees—200 out of 2,000—were all at the bottom rung, although the company had no overt biases. Upon further examination, it developed that Negroes stayed at the bottom because they never took the written exams which the company used to measure qualifications for promotion; they simply assumed that the tests were designed to give the company an excuse for not promoting them. Since the tests bore little relation to the job functions involved, the president ordered them replaced with job-performance tests and on-the-job training.

The article tells us that as a result, seventy Negroes were upgraded. Apparently, then, we must reexamine corporate testing procedures in order to hire more Negroes. One executive feels that for a number of positions on-the-job training can be given Negroes who fail the usual qualifying tests.

If business does decide to go all out for Negro employment, other problems may arise, even if the Negroes meet the full employment requirements. Types of job assignments present one problem. The sales area presents another, particularly when the consumer group is predominantly white. We all know the problems presented by geography. Those of us who have clients spread throughout the country know that deep-rooted practices and customs will not be changed overnight.

But we must, of course, as thoughtful citizens, try to help change those practices and customs. We know that new minority employees in work groups may cause some disruption for a short time. But those of us who have had the experience of introducing Negroes into a group of white workers for the first time have seen that many of our so-called "fears" were groundless. It is a matter of taking the initiative, going ahead and making the move, despite our fears at the outset.

Employee recreation programs sometimes present a problem. One company in a large city in a border state, for example, must have two annual summer picnics because no park in the area can be used for a picnic for both colored and white employees. This is the way it is at the moment—but certainly we have to work toward the day when there can be one picnic for all employees.

We also discussed union agreements, and many reported on their experience in trying to modify some of the contractual provisions, particularly in agreements made in the South, which, in fact, established colored locals. In one case where a Negro local was to be disbanded, the Negroes themselves objected, because by giving up their local autonomy they lost representation at the state or national conferences. Again business must take the initiative because the unions will not. Business will also have to take the initiative to include nondiscrimination clauses in contracts that do not have them. And business will have to take the initiative to permit the upgrading of Negroes through the normal progression of seniority.

After a discussion of various problem areas, our group presented a summary of the constructive ideas advanced:

1. Additional training for unsuccessful applicants. This might include night courses, possibly with the assistance of government agencies. Work in this direction is well under way.

2. The counseling of Negroes in the community so that they might develop more ambition to qualify for jobs that may be available in industry.

3. On-the-job upgrading training programs. These programs need a special push from leaders of minority groups, who must make it clear that the Negro must strive to improve himself. In this connection we should support community programs aimed at developing youth motivation.

4. Intensification of our efforts to convince the Negro community that as responsible leaders of industry, we are serious in our intent.

5. Extended programs of in-service education of supervisors. We have a long way to go in this direction because of the belief among supervisory people that the Negro, because of his lack of advantages and opportunity to learn, is not as efficient as the white person.

6. The coordination among personnel management associations of information about opportunities for employment of Negroes. The services of the private employment agencies that have grown during the last few years and that specialize in seeking out and referring capable Negro applicants to industry can also be used.

We concluded that we must review again our selection techniques in order to give the Negro a fair opportunity for employment in industry, that we must engage in internal company development programs that will upgrade the Negroes who are employed and open the door for unemployed Negroes, and that we must then urge the Negro community itself to do more to improve the skills and capabilities of the Negroes.

Initially, the members of our group were looking for immediate answers to current problems. It soon became clear, however, that the first and foremost problem is to recognize the reality of the situation. This has two aspects: first, we must recognize that all through the management organizations and companies we represent, enthusiasm at one level becomes acquiescence at the next level and resistance at the third. The workers at this last level can ruin any plan that management wants to establish if they are not in sympathy with it.

Next, we must recognize the problem of the companies themselves. Business cannot solve this problem alone, but there are some steps it can take. This is *not* just a social problem that is to be coped with by government or by social workers; it is a matter of fundamental justice and morality. Practical businessmen must recognize that this is a deep-seated economic problem that threatens every business, perhaps even our business system.

First, certain situations are so explosive that they could well erupt into violence, even bloodshed. Business cannot tolerate such disturbance. Business could be brought to a virtual standstill in such an atmosphere, as indeed it has in many parts of the world. Second, it is cheaper to educate and train people than to pay for relief or prison upkeep. This is a simple economic fact. Third, the political realities are such that restrictions, legislation, and the direction of business could bring an end to what we call free enterprise.

Finally, businessmen are accustomed to dealing with risks, and this is a matter of risk taking, where the risk of doing something seems to be substantially less than the risk of doing nothing. To bring about an understanding of the situation will involve some individual effort on the part of those who have their own organizations. It will require extensive effort outside these companies. It will require more conferences and the efforts of trade associations and similar groups.

Essentially, we need to develop a belief, a conviction, that something can and should be done, and since this must be done throughout an organization, it must evolve into action and not lip service. It is a part of an action effort. There should be a simple recognition that if we start treating Negroes as intelligent, responsible human beings, they will learn to act and react like responsible human beings—but we must take the first step. We cannot wait for them to become educated—we cannot wait for them to become responsible—we cannot wait for them to take the first step—*we* must take the first step.

The action and interaction of people dictate that, if a desire to accomplish a certain end can be widely inculcated, the results will be that end.

We discussed many ways of accomplishing this end, including training programs. One effort is worth mentioning: a system of recruitment that involves record keeping and follow-up, active recruitment at Negro colleges and at high schools, a statement to the schools of what education is required for various jobs, the provision of applicant tests so that the schools themselves can train people for that test, and a program of on-the-job training for advancement.

In another program that has been followed for six or seven years a company has encouraged its people, all down the line, to participate in affairs in their own communities. They have encouraged them to serve on the board of the Urban League and to help the high schools with their drop-out problems. As one example, they took ninety children with a D average, who according to the teachers were destined to be drop-outs, and in sixteen weeks of training, brought the average of the group up to B+. This is a significant demonstration, a clear-cut example of what can be done.

On one matter it was difficult to attain agreement—the matter of preferential treatment. On this question, opinions ranged from a belief that minimum standards must be preserved, even though they may block the hiring of some Negroes, to a contention that the policies must have some elasticity. The group as a whole however was fairly well persuaded that an organization must follow the practice of treating all workers once employed and once trained with equality, and this includes not only advancement but also firing and other discipline.

We also agreed that we must expect, and we must teach our organizations to expect, to be discouraged when our best efforts seem to result in nothing more than increased demands and more friction. We must not be upset when one plant in a company that is doing a good job over-all happens to be the target of a demonstration.

Finally, we agreed that educators, social workers, government, and the Negro community itself must not expect the manufacturing industries to solve the problem alone or entirely or expect manufacturing to render itself inefficient in an attempt to solve the problem, for this would succeed only in national degradation. We do not believe any answer will ever be found if we attempt to solve the problem by emasculating the economic strength of the nation as it exists. Manufacturing should and can be expected to do substantially more of what might be its share.

One real solution was suggested: to create entirely new industries, probably in the service field, where there is a great opportunity. One can look at any problem as an opportunity, and here certainly is a great opportunity for creative entrepreneurship. Nevertheless, while manufacturing can and should be expected to do more than its share, it by no means can do the whole job alone.

In the fourth group everyone exhibited a strong desire to solve the problem that is facing us. In view of this, it is indeed likely that American industry will accomplish this goal. Surely those who shared in this conference have made strides.

The group centered its attention on certain problem areas.

In the crucial area of employment we agreed with the solutions already mentioned, namely, to hire more qualified Negroes and to hire others for training. Our group also debated the question of preferential selection. Some felt that a wrong will not correct a wrong; others, that we might practice preferential selection but we must differentiate between selection and recruitment. Actually, some companies today are exerting extra effort in the recruiting of qualified Negroes, and this might seem to contradict the contention that preference is wrong. Nevertheless, extra effort is being applied in the recruiting of Negro personnel not only at the college level but also among those who currently hold jobs.

This subject includes, of course, training and education. It involves internal training as well as training in the community. In each instance the proper course of action for individual companies must be determined by its capabilities and by its size and status or situation in a community. Training was considered to be not strictly an industrial problem. In fact, one point of view was that the necessary training is much too extensive for industry to handle and that the government will have to undertake the task.

We discussed the cost of unemployment and were advised of the large numbers of people who will be coming into the labor market in the next few years, as well as the numbers already in the unemployed ranks today. This is a problem that industry will have to cope with, and it could become more costly than necessary if we do not pay attention to it.

We discussed the available resources and techniques for reaching the Negro community, or the Negro himself, among them, the use of Negro agencies and of advertising in Negro newspapers and magazines. Several companies are using consultants for recruitment research as well as for public relations, which goes beyond the immediate community in many cases but is specifically directed to the organizations, schools, churches, and neighborhoods in the Negro community. Some companies have specifically employed Negroes to work in the areas of sales, marketing, and advertising related to a Negro public.

One member suggested the publication of an Aids to Industry that would display case studies or histories of successful programs. It was also resolved unanimously that all the talks presented formally at this conference be compiled and published for our use, a recommendation that was intended as a specific step in assisting industry to solve its particular problem.

Another fact we confronted was that, although we might not agree to it or accept it, CORE and NAACP are attempting in some communities to bring pressure on industry. These organizations, however, can themselves contribute to our attempts to solve our problems and the community's problems. They can help lay the groundwork for programs and actions that are directed to the over-all problem. We should, however, be cautious of those groups that exhibit coercive action or pressure techniques, for we must be certain they are acting in the best interest of the community as well the company or industry.

We must also remember that our actions today and tomorrow might relate to problems that come up at the negotiating table with the unions. If we take the fair and right steps now problems will be removed that might otherwise be used at the bargaining table.

We agreed, in summary, that if we accept the facts of integration, of true integration, and work at it consistently and earnestly, taking each problem as it comes up, we will, in the long run if not the short, be able to solve the problem amicably and not allow it to evolve into widespread disruption. A sound company or corporate policy must start at the top if it is to be successful at all, and in order to insure compliance, there must be a true follow-up system, not just a cursory review. Integration can ultimately be made to work; in fact, it will prove to be less of a stumbling block than many of us make it appear today.

THE CORPORATION AND THE COMMUNITY

In this concluding chapter the resource personnel who had an opportunity to participate in the several sessions of the Conference made some concluding comments on four phases of the problem: on the stance that corporations could adopt; on the specific techniques and operating procedures available to them; on continuing relationships between the business and the Negro community; and finally on the responsibilities of American business to the advancement of a democratic society.

THE CORPORATION STANCE

Dale L. Hiestand

It seems clear that there was a definitely favorable consensus on the whole question of integration and the enlargement of employment opportunities for Negroes. The question that remained unresolved concerned the desirability of preferential treatment.

Some members of the conference felt that preferential treatment is immoral or unethical—that we cannot accomplish good ends by changing to a system which unfairly discriminates against others, in this case, white workers.

There was strong resistance to any sort of a system that would result in bringing in incompetent people. Some raised questions about the cost of such a system. For organizations that are in competitive situations, this poses a real problem.

Others felt that this question depended on the economic strength of the organization. Still others who would not accept the principle of preference said they would do many things in practice including bending the rules one way or another, but they wanted to preserve the principle in order not to have to engage in a counterfight at some time in the future.

The answers seemed to turn on semantics. Some people wanted to try special programs, to work on compensatory measures, to make extra efforts to seek out the really qualified. There is an effort under way, and there will be a continuing effort, to find ways of doing something effective for minority groups that can be carried back to top management for its support.

One aspect of the testing situation, however, might be considered. Historically, business made relatively little use of testing procedures, preferring for many years more haphazard methods of selection: whom the employee knew, for example, or who his friends were, or who happened to walk in through the gate. Suddenly, at the same time that the Negro is beginning to be accepted, business has begun to use elaborate testing systems. Consequently, Negroes find themselves being assessed by different rules from those used in the past, and Negro organizations and individuals can legitimately question current testing and selection procedures. This raises the possibility, at least, that as business reexamines its testing procedures it will discover a great deal, not only about how these procedures affect Negro applicants, but how they operate with respect to white applicants and employees as well. Perhaps the whole system will be improved.

TECHNIQUES AND PROCEDURES

John G. Feild

A very considerable body of excellent professional, technical knowledge on how to deal with this problem has been developed in this Conference. We discussed techniques in assignment, selection, recruiting, how to motivate the minority employees who have been underutilized, and how to involve them in important development programs.

One of the problems we still face, again in a technical sense, is that we have not yet reached a point where we can draw together that body of knowledge and the body of experience that has been growing out of industry so that it can be readily and effectively transmitted to other practitioners. Soon, however, we will begin to collate this information and draw it together in a systematic fashion, thereby saving enormous amounts of time when these problems come up at different locations. This is uniquely the responsibility of the societies and associations that have grown up to serve industry. In particular, personnel managers may come to be far more important in this area than they have been in the past.

Already, governmental agencies have drawn together a substantial body of knowledge and experience. Curiously, the best of that body of experience happens to be in those agencies that are regulators, not the educators or business-supporting groups. For example, the Department of Commerce has done very little to serve industry in this area, and yet this is that agency of government that one would expect to have been most helpful with respect to the problems and conditions that industry faced. Perhaps some kind of pressure, request, or channel of communication needs to be developed and initiated by business groups to obtain such service from government.

BUSINESS AND THE NEGRO COMMUNITY

Joseph P. Lyford

One difficulty the American business executive faces in dealing with the Negro is that he has rarely taken the trouble to learn anything about the interior of the Negro community—its leadership, its prejudices, its way of doing things, its inconsistencies. In fact, his ignorance of the Negro individually and collectively is part of a pattern of unawareness that extends to any alienated segment of our society. Consequently, the growing number of business executives who are making a conscientious effort to recognize the rights and demands of ethnic minorities in employment find themselves bewildered and frustrated when they begin to deal with the problem. Seated for the first time at a table with a Negro delegation, they find that they do not even know whether to use the word "Negro" or "colored," and this is only the beginning of their floundering and embarrassment. Inevitably, the businessmen who sit down to a conference table with nothing but good intentions will end by having to be led when they should be leading.

The corporate executive badly needs an education about the Negro in his local community and in history so as to develop some ability to examine situations from the Negro's point of view. He is not likely to develop this new viewpoint simply by sitting down with delegations from CORE or the NAACP to discuss proposals and hear grievances. For without some comprehension of the Negro community, he will simply react to such confrontations in terms of his own administrative conveniences and preoccupations. The meaning behind the Negroes' language will be completely lost on him.

Once the corporation executive recognizes that the interest of his company requires action, it would seem reasonable to expect him to anticipate and plan creatively instead of simply to react to minimum demands and make the wayside concessions

so typical of defensive management's dealings with Negro employment and promotion. Business has not usually advanced on
the problem and grasped all its implications at the outset. Rather,
it has ordinarily backed into the situation, conceding instead of
proposing, retreating instead of initiating, and making future
negotiation inevitable.

The most promising place to begin is away from the negotiating
table, as management has discovered in its dealings with organized labor. Here the conversation can begin long before a
situation has reached the stage of demand and counterdemand.
When I hear business executives relate their problems in trying
to "compromise" with the Negro community, I am reminded of
my own experience as chairman of a local political organization.
The members of my political committee, drawn from many different economic and religious sectors of the community, used
to arrive at each monthly meeting filled with hearsay about each
other and committed, with ferocious determination, to do each
other in, no matter what the issues to be discussed. One group
would wait until another had announced its position on an issue
so as to be sure to come out for the opposite point of view. This
animosity existed because members of the opposing groups never
associated or talked with each other except at monthly policy
meetings. By planning committee gatherings that were primarily
social, rather than political, we managed to dissipate some of
this hostility. Once people had a chance to establish some basis
for a relationship other than pure group politics, they began to
understand each other and to lose some of their personal dis-
trust, even though they often continued to disagree on political
issues.

If business is to act positively toward the Negro community,
there must be something more than negotiations. This advice
applies to other white groups that dominate American life. The
New England, the Middle Western, the Northern metropolitan
white communities still regard the Negro community as a foreign
colony, a fact too obvious to dwell upon. Burdened by this attitude, white groups go about trying to deal with questions that

involve white and Negro relationships as if they were on diplo-
matic missions or technical errands. Serious crises in human
relationships are not resolved by correspondence; nor can any
computer provide a satisfactory formula for settlement. Neither
the Negro's vocabulary, his needs, nor his temper can be estimated at long distance. This simply means that business executives will have to be personally involved with the Negro and his
community, as learners, not lecturers or sight-seers. Negotiating
with civil rights groups on employment may be good in-service
training for white executives but it is no more than an elementary
step, and the advice of a Negro personnel manager or corporation
vice president on race relations is not a satisfactory substitute for
management's own education.

Many businessmen, once they have made "concessions," find
that new demands are made of them. This is natural. Where
the Negro succeeds in opening up employment and promotion
opportunities, he will apply greater and greater pressure for
more until he has achieved full equality. The businessman who
makes "concessions" under pressure then asks, "When will they
stop? How far will the civil rights people go?" The question
need never have been asked had these same businessmen acted
on their own initiative, with some imagination and understanding.
Concessions that have to be extracted by pressure are seldom
appreciated and they never satisfy. The white business executive
should consider the issue of Negro employment from the
Negro's angle. The more progress the executive makes, the more
progress he should seek. In other words, he could become a little
more competitive about success in his dealing with the Negro.

I see no sensible argument against an intelligent effort to raise
the hopes of the Negro by giving him all the opportunities he
can use. We cannot complain about apathetic, unqualified
Negroes on the one hand and on the other make no positive effort
to dissolve their apathy and improve their ability to work. One
thing is certain: the business executive who simply responds to
a prodding or a poking will spend the rest of his business career

being prodded and poked until he backs over a cliff of his own making.

A corporation that waits to be approached by the Negro leadership is already in trouble; it has already been judged delinquent, and this creates the worst possible atmosphere for negotiation. The corporation may also find itself forced to deal with five or six different organizations, some of which cannot be identified or assessed, each with different demands and different motives. One way of avoiding this confusion is to learn something about the leadership of the Negro community before a crisis develops. While in some cases the civil rights leaders in a specific city may have shown excessive rigidity and hostility, it is generally unwise to attempt to bypass the recognized leadership in favor of more tractable Negro "spokesmen." Even if more satisfactory settlements can be made with the tractable spokesmen, they are not likely to be ratified by the opinion of the Negro community.

The failure of businessmen generally to establish a social as well as political relationship with Negro communities explains, in part, the emphasis in management–civil rights negotiations on techniques and temporary adjustments rather than long-range programs. The corporation that becomes mired in half-programs or half-solutions will never be free of the problem; it will eventually learn what it is to be "nibbled to death by a duck," as a veteran labor reporter once described the process of perpetual negotiation. So perhaps we might put techniques in their proper secondary place. A businessman who wants to move forward will have relatively little difficulty developing the means to reach his objective. What is important is that he have an objective.

The business executive's approach to the Negro will be affected by the community in which they meet. It obviously makes a difference whether a corporation is in Tennessee or Illinois or New Hampshire, or whether it is in a small town or a large city. Geography, however, does not alter the fact that if businessmen are to get over their sense of harassment they will have to learn, along with other white Americans, that it will not be enough to reach the stage where they can say, "Well, now, the Negro has his freedom and a job; he can vote without hindrance and exercise all his other constitutional rights—and that's the end of the matter." There is no peace in the future if black and white Americans exclude each other from their own societies and try to live in peaceful coexistence. Separate but equal races is as full of future turmoil as separate but equal schools. We will still have to deal with a racial wall of cold, hard psychological and social attitudes—in some ways more dangerous to us than the Berlin wall is to the Germans because of the simple fact that we built our walls ourselves, while their wall was forced on them. Our racial walls will have to be breached and the American businessman must help in the demolition.

THE RESPONSIBILITY OF AMERICAN BUSINESS

Oscar Cohen

Basic decisions must be made in the business community in social, economic, and political affairs as they relate to the Negro crisis. An essential question to be answered is whether or not business should be involved in broad community problems. In other words, should the business community deal with matters going far beyond those directly related to the sale and production of products, hiring, upgrading, and training. In this context three propositions should be considered.

The first proposition is that business in the United States has overwhelming power. This is a myth, although it is widely believed. The business establishment does not run the United States; it does not elect the Congress of the United States; and while it has substantial power, it cannot change or mold society at will.

Second, business has become increasingly community-conscious. Business corporations have become involved in the welfare of society and are deeply concerned with problems of race. There seems to be an increasing acceptance of the contention that what is good for the United States is good for General Motors.

Third, industry cannot operate efficiently in a society in conflict. Therefore industry has a large stake in the avoidance of racial strife, a stake which might motivate industry to look beyond its plant or office doors and into the general community.

In discussions among business leaders the question has been raised, to what extent should industry be involved in the national education process? There was general agreement that our schools do not satisfactorily meet the needs of industry. There was also general agreement that the schools need to be told wherein they are failing to meet these needs and that industry has a responsibility to advise them. As we have heard, some companies have provided the schools with the tests that they use in screening for employment, to serve as a guide for vocational training. In some areas industry is providing opportunity for in-plant education in the afternoon for youngsters who go to school in the morning. Corporations lend staff to high schools and colleges for the teaching of classes. Some industries report tuition aid, whereby a percentage of the cost of training is borne by corporate funds. Tutorial projects are frequently sponsored by industry, sometimes not directly related to training for a particular industry. In some cases executives are being encouraged to become members of school boards. This involvement of the business leader on a personal basis involves the corporation, which approves or actively supports such action. There is corporate involvement in general scholarship funds and in particular funds such as the Negro scholarship funds.

Industry, in short, is already involved in a wide complex of educational matters.

The question is asked, however, to what extent should industry go out of its way to become further involved? In some cases, if involvement is to be effective, there may be political overtones because of local, state, and Federal support for education.

While there is a fair amount of agreement on the role of business in education, there are other problems on which there are substantially different points of view. For example, what effort should be made by business through trade associations and other means to effect employment opportunities for Negroes? What kinds of action, if any, should be undertaken by industry through its formal organizations to assure social agreement in the nation and to help the civil rights movement? In this area there seems to be a somewhat timid approach.

There is still less agreement on what should be done about circumstances in the community at large which affect community-industry relationships. Take housing as an example. If an industry wishes to move personnel freely, the community climate is of vital significance. Cases have been cited of industries wishing to move qualified Negro personnel to areas in which decent housing for them is unavailable. In such cases, some argue, housing must be a concern of the business community and one which cannot be solved without involvement in community affairs in an effort to exert influence. The free use of recreational and other facilities is also relevant. Sit-downs at restaurants or other places of business become part of the racial strife that hinders business and makes certain areas unattractive to key personnel. It is important to note that strife-ridden areas are shunned not only by Negroes but also by many intelligent, sensitive white employees.

Attitudes toward involvement of business in the civil rights movement are varied. There is anxiety over the extent, if any, to which business concerns should contribute corporate funds to support the movements. It seems to be generally agreed that funds for the Urban League are desirable. But there are other civil rights movements of varying degrees of militancy where support may have questionable value. One company, we have been told, passed the word down that it was desirable in the eyes of management for executives to become part of community-sponsored and, in some cases, city-wide or state-wide civil rights groups. Experience indicates that the industry representative who serves on such boards as a public relations gesture can produce the reverse effect. In those cases where industry representatives apply the thinking and genius of American industry to the pro-lems, a contribution can be made of great significance in pro-moting community harmony and progress.

The hardest question to answer pertains to legislation. It is not unknown, of course, for industry to lobby for or against certain legislation. That being the case, should industry lobby for such matters as Federal civil rights measures? This can be a salient question since business has a stake in avoiding com-munity and national conflict.

Many believe the march on Washington prevented violence in 1963. Industry has a great stake in the civil rights legislation, even though it may be bothered by some of their provisions, but passage will not end the quest for legislation on this issue. The problem will be a recurrent one. Industry is also concerned with legislation that pertains to full employment. It has been stated that unless industrial leaders take some constructive steps in this direction, it will be done for them.

In the discussions among business leaders here, horizons seem to have become higher as talks progressed. Increasingly execu-tives have come to think of their industries as not merely pro-ducers and sellers of products, but as a part of a society in which they have broad responsibilities.

The changes during the last ten years in attitudes, action, and leadership, all so well exemplified at this conference, argue well for national progress and avoidance of conflict. All participants have agreed that there is trouble ahead, but the attitudes ex-pressed by business leaders and the considerable talent and experience they are bringing to bear on problems of racial in-equality are cause for optimism.

Index

Catalog

If you are interested in a list of fine Paperback
books, covering a wide range of subjects
and interests, send your name and address,
requesting your free catalog, to:

McGraw-Hill Paperbacks
330 West 42nd Street
New York, New York 10036